Origins and Development
of the
Second Amendment

Origins and Development
of the
Second Amendment

by

David T. Hardy

PUBLISHERS
BLACKSMITH
CORPORATION

Hardy, David T.
Origins and Development of the Second Amendment.

Bibliography: p.
1. Firearms—Law and legislation—United States.
2. Civil rights—United States. I. Title
KF3941.H37 1986   344.73'0533   86-14735
ISBN 0-941540-13-8   344.304533

TABLE OF CONTENTS

A THOUSAND YEARS DEVELOPING: ARMS BEARING BEFORE 1640

THE CRUCIAL HALF-CENTURY: 1639-1689

"By God, not for an hour!": The English Civil War

Restoration and Disarmament: 1660

"An Abominable Thing, To Disarm the Nation": The Glorious Revolution and the Declaration of Rights

AN ARMED PEOPLE: PROLOGUE TO REVOLUTION

Universal Gun Ownership as a Legal Duty: The Colonial Militia Laws

The Whigs and American Political Perception

APPEAL TO ARMS: THE AMERICAN REVOLUTION

The Road to Revolution

A NATIONAL CONSTITUTION — BUT NO BILL OF RIGHTS

A Federalist View

The AntiFederalist View

The State Conventions Demand a Bill of Rights

THE DRAFTING OF THE BILL OF RIGHTS

CONTEMPORARY DISCUSSIONS OF THE SECOND AMENDMENT

THE RIGHT TO KEEP AND BEAR ARMS IN THE COURTS

What is the Nature of the Right?

The Right to Bear Arms in the Supreme Court

ACKNOWLEDGEMENTS

In the seven years of research which preceded this work, I received a variety of assistance and encouragement. To my parents, Albert and Madeline Hardy, I owe the initial suggestion that what had hitherto been casual notes be assembled into a book. My wife, Frances, a medieval historian by training, gave appreciation and encouragement whch began (if I remember correctly) with our second date. Robert Dowlut, a second amendment authority in his own right, spent long hours to give the manuscript a detailed proof reading. Mary Kaaren Jolly, then a counsel to the Senate Judiciary Committee, gave further impetus to the work by persuading the Committee to employ the research in a 1982 report. I join with all other current second amendment commentators in a collective debt — "joint and several" in nature — to Joyce Malcom's groundbreaking work on the right to keep and bear arms in 17th century England, and Steve Halbrook's work on the right on 18th century America. I owe a more specific debt to Washington and Lee University, the Thomas Jefferson Memorial Foundation which maintains Monticello, and the James Monroe Museum of Fredericksburg, for authorization to photograph the firearms of Washington, Jefferson, and Monroe.

Finally, I should acknowledge the assistance of Mark William Hardy, who arrived in the world during the preparation of this manuscript. Without his aid, its completion would have been measurably delayed by the drive to sleep; to him, it is dedicated.

INTRODUCTION

When our first Congress drafted the Bill of Rights in 1789, the rights it singled out for mention may have been inalienable, but for the most part they were hardly ancient. A student of the history of freedom of speech and press, for instance, would have found it a very brief study. Until 1695 publication of a book on politics, history, religion or science required a government permit; in 1680, a royal judge had not hesitated to warn publishers that "to print or publish any news books or pamphlets of any kind is illegal". When Parliament listed the rights of Englishmen in 1688, these restrictions on the press did not merit a mention. Freedom to assemble and petition the government had still less of a pedigree. The 1661 Act Against Tumultuous Petitioning had made it illegal to petition the King without an appropriate permit; a group of citizens who in 1701 politely presented a mild petition to Parliament, seeking passage of a budget bill, were imprisoned on the spot. (E.N. Williams, Eighteenth Century Constitution 410-11 (1960)). Freedom to practice religion, and from establishment of a religion, were hardly keystones of the common law. Their recognition in the first amendment is largely the result of James Madison's exposure to the colonial custom of imprisoning non-Anglican ministers for preaching without a licence. To be sure, not all the rights commemorated in 1789 were novelties. Claims to a right against self-incrimination had been made with some frequency in Elizabethan times, and trial by jury (albeit not always an impartial one) had been traditional for several centuries. Yet even these origins are unimpressive when judged by the standards of the oldest right of them all—the right to keep and bear arms.

Like its younger cousin, the right to trial by jury, the right to keep and bear arms can first be seen as a duty to keep and bear arms. But when, sometime in the twelfth century, the English were required to serve on juries and ferret out criminals, they had already been required for a dozen or more generations to own and use arms. It is hardly surprising that these universal duties became a way of life and a mainstay of their political consensus, and in turn became, when such things began to be debated, a right. To a person of the age of Jefferson and Madison, this history would have been no revelation: a solid grasp of history was in their age deemed essential to the most basic legal studies. Today, of course, matters are different...thus, this work.

A THOUSAND YEARS DEVELOPING: ARMS BEARING BEFORE 1640

"Every landowner was obliged to keep armor and weapons according to his rank and possessions; these he might neither sell, lend, nor pledge, nor even alienate from his heirs."

To the generation of 1789, legal training began and often ended with the commentaries of the great William Blackstone, from whom they learned that "It seems universally agreed by all historians that King Alfred first settled a national militia in this kingdom, and by his prudent discipline made all the subjects of his dominion soldiers..." (Commentaries, Bk.I, ch. XIII). To trace a right to Alfred—who, after all, died in 899 A.D.—is no mean feat. Yet more recent historians have traced the individual legal duty to own arms and be skilled in their use to 690 A.D., and concluded that it is in fact "older than our oldest records." (J. Bagley & P. Rowly, A Documentary History of England, Vol.I, at 152). Here, at a point closer to the time of Julius Ceasar than that of Thomas Jefferson, lies the origin of our own second amendment.

1. SAXON LAWS OF ARMS BEARING:500-1066 A.D.

The Saxons, a germanic tribe, invaded Britain between the fifth and seventh centuries and dominated the island until the Norman conquest of 1066. The account which follows reflects what was known of their military customs at the birth of our own nation. Their customs are of especial interest since colonial writers—including Thomas Paine and Thomas Jefferson—were fond of citing the Saxons as a sort of English 'Noble Savage' whose noble yet democratic systems were crushed by the 'Norman Yoke'.

> By the Saxon laws, every freeman of an age capable of bearing arms, and not incapacitated by any bodily infirmity, was in case of a foreign invasion, internal insurrection, or other emergency, obliged to join the army.... Every landowner was obliged to keep armor and weapons according to his rank and possessions; these he might neither sell, lend, nor pledge, nor even alienate from his heirs. In order to instruct them in the use of arms, they had their stated times for performing their military exercise; and once in a year, generally in the spring, there was a general review of arms, throughout each county.

(Francis Grose, Military Antiquities Respecting a History of the English Army, at 1-2 (London, 1812))

2. THE ASSIZE OF ARMS: 1181

In 1066, the Saxon kingdoms fell to William the Conqueror, Duke of Normandy. William imported with him the Norman feudal system—the most advanced of its kind—and imposed it in England. Landowners generally held their land from the king, or from each other, in consideration of 'Knight's Fees', each fee representing a duty to provide one knight for 40 days' service per year. The new dynasty did not, however, abandon the Saxon concept of universal arms bearing.

In 1181, Henry II proclaimed the Assize of Arms—'Assize' then meaning, among other things, a form of statute. While in continental Europe, society was divided largely into a heavily-armed nobility and a disarmed peasantry, in England every free man (i.e. everyone not a serf) had to buy arms, and his feudal lord was forbidden to take them, even as a gift!

> Whosoever holds one knight's fee shall have a coat of mail, a helmet, a shield and a lance; and every knight as many...as he shall have knight's fees in his domain. Every free layman having in chattels (moveable property) or rent (lands) to the value of 15 marks, shall keep a coat of mail, a helmet and shield and a lance. Every free layman who shall have in chattels or rent 10 marks, shall have a habergon (sleeveless armored coat), a chaplet (skullcap) of iron and a lance. Also all burgesses and the whole community of freemen shall have a wambais (inexpensive leather body armor), a chaplet of iron, and a lance. Every one of these shall swear that he will have these arms before the Feast of St. Hillary...and no man having these arms shall sell, pledge, nor lend them, nor alienate them in any manner; nor shall the Lord take them from his vassal by forfeiture, gift, pledge, or any other manner.

(Francis Grose, Military Antiquities Respecting a History of the English Army, at 1-2 (London, 1812))

3. THE STATUTE OF WINCHESTER, 1285

In 1285, complaining that "robberies, murders, burnings and theft, be more often used than they have been heretofore," Edward I ordered a variety of anti-crime measures. The statute pressured local juries to apprehend criminals, established night watches with absolute powers of arrest, and ordered clearing of all brush two hundred feet on either side of highways, to prevent ambush. Far from trying to control crime by restricting weapons, the statute actually broadened the Assize of Arms. Now 'every man'—not just 'every free man' had a legal duty to obtain arms!

> And further, it is commanded that every man have in his house Harness (armor) for to keep the peace after the antient Assize; that is to say, Every man between fifteen years of age and sixty

years of age shall be assessed and sworn to armor according to the quantity of their Lands and Goods; that is, to wit, from Fifteen Pounds Lands and Goods Forty Marks, an Hauberke of iron, a sword, a knife and a horse....and he that hath less than Forty Shillings yearly, shall be sworn to keep Gisarmes (a pole-ax), knives and other less weapons...and all others that may, shall have Bowes and Arrows...

(13 Edw. I c.1)

4. THE STATUTE OF NORTHAMPTON: LIMITS ON THE BEARING OF ARMS

Edward III promulgated the Statute of Northampton in a time of severe political upheaval. (To be precise, he was then being held prisoner by his father's murderer, whom he later overthrew and executed: 14th century politics was a risky business). The statute barred carrying of arms in riots ('affrays') and in certain places such as courts. On its face, it also appeared to allow riding armed 'in no place elsewhere'. As the selection which follows this makes clear, however, the statute was read only to prohibit carrying of unusual arms for purposes of creating terror.

Item, it is enacted, that no man great or small, of whatever condition soever he be, except the King's servants in his presence,...and also upon a cry for arms to keep the peace, and the same in such places where such acts happen, be so hardy as to come before the King's Justices, or other of the King's ministers doing their office, with force and arms, nor bring no force in affray of the peace, nor to go nor ride armed by night nor by day, in fairs, markets, nor in the presence of the Justices or other Ministers, nor in no part elsewhere....

(2 Edward III c.3, 1328)

5. AN ENGLISH COURT CONSTRUES THE STATUTE OF NORTHAMPTON

Reports of early English cases differ greatly from their modern counterparts, having been prepared by private persons who listened to the decision and made their notes. This particular decision is actually reported twice—at 87 Eng. Rep. 75 and at 90 Eng. Rep. 330, each report giving a different insight. The critical portions of each are set forth below. 'Desuetude' is an argument that a statute has lapsed by being long ignored in practice; 'connivance' at this time indicated an intent to tolerate (literally, to wink at) actions; 'malo animo' designated an 'evil mind' or illegal intent.

> Information for going to church with pistols, etc., contra stat. 2 Edw. 3, of Northampton. Winnington pro defendente. This statute was made to prevent the people's being oppressed by great men, but this is a private matter, and not within the statute. Vide stat. 20 R. 2.
>
> The offense had been much greater, and better laid at common law. But tho' this statute be almost gone in desuetudinem, yet where the crime shall appear to be malo animo, it will come within the act (tho' there now be a general connivance to gentlemen to ride armed for their security); but afterward he was found not guilty.
>
> ....
>
> The information sets forth that the defendant did walk about the streets armed with guns, and that he went into the Church of St. Michael, in Bristol, in the time of divine service, with a gun, to terrify the King's subjects, contrast formam statuti. The case was tried at the bar, and the defendant was acquitted. The chief justice said, that the meaning of the statute of 2 Edw. 3,c.3, was to punish people who go armed to terrify the King's subjects.

(Sir John Knight's Case, 87 Eng. Rep. 75, 90 Eng. Rep. 330 (King's Bench, 1687))

6. HENRY VII PROHIBITS SHOOTING OF CROSSBOWS

By the fifteenth century, English kings had become enamoured with a particular weapon—the longbow. Firing armor-piercing arrows, drawn by a man constantly trained in its use (many such bows had a pull well over a hundred pounds), the longbow smashed French and Scottish armies. To encourage skill in its use, English kings built target ranges, fixed bow prices, and outlawed virtually all sports and games except archery. In 1503, apparently finding that many persons were experimenting with crossbow shooting, Henry VII restricted it...not because the crossbow was too deadly for commoners, but because it was not deadly enough! In the following selection the spelling has been modernized from that found in the Statutes ("Theking oure souaigne Lorde...")

> The King our sovereign Lord, considering right well that in the time of his most noble progenitor shooting in longbows has been much used in this, his realm, whereby honor and victory have been gotten against enemies and the realm greatly defended...which shooting is now greatly decayed in the realm, since of late the King's subjects greatly delight themselves in using crossbows, whereby great destruction of the king's deer as well in forest chases as in parks daily is had and done, and shooting in longbows little or nothing used and likely in short space to be lost and utterly decayed, to the great hurt and enfeebling of this realm and to the comfort of our outward enemies.... hath ordained and enacted, that after the feast of Easter coming next no person within this realm, without the king's special license under his placard signed and sealed with his privy seal or signet, shall occupy or shoot in any crossbow, unless he shoot out of a house for the lawful defense of the same, except he be a Lord or that he...have lands...to the yearly value of 200 Marks....

(19 Hen.VII c.4)

7. HENRY VIII RENEWS THE STATUTE OF WINCHESTER

In 1512, Henry VIII acted to expand the Statute of Winchester. Not only were all adult males to be armed, but children were to be armed with bows by their parents, bow makers were to produce bows of less expensive woods, and cities were to provide target ranges ('butts').

> Every man being the King's subject, not lame, decrepit, or maimed, nor having any other lawful or reasonable cause or impediment, being within the age of sixty years (is required) to use and exercise shooting in longbows, and also to have a bow and arrows ready continually in his house to use himself in shooting;

and also that the father, governors, and rulers of such as be of tender age do teach them and bring them up in the knowledge of the same shooting; and every man having a man child or men children in his house shall provide ordinance…for every child being of the age of seven years and above 'till he come to the age of seventeen years a bow and four shafts to amuse them and learn them and bring them up in shooting….and that every bowyer within this realm always make for every bow of yew that he makes to sell four bows of elm or other wood of mean price …and also that butts be made in every city, town and place according to the law of ancient time use, and that the inhabitants and dwellers in every of them be compelled to make and continue such butts and exercise themselves with the longbow in shooting at the same and elsewhere on holidays and other times convenient.

(3 Hen. VIII c.3)

8. HENRY ATTEMPTS TO BAN HANDGUN SHOOTING

Like his father, Henry was concerned that crossbows and other weapons might divert his subjects from practice with what he considered the more deadly longbow. In 1511 he revived his father's ban on crossbow shooting. In 1514, he attempted to ban shooting of handguns, which at that time included any firearm fired by hand (i.e., smaller than a cannon). Here, also, the spelling has been modernized.

Whereas the King's subjects daily delight themselves in the shooting of crossbows, whereby shooting in longbows is the less used, and diverse good statutes for the reformation of the same have been made and had, and that, nowithstanding, many and diverse not regarding nor fearing the penalties of the said statutes used daily to shoot in crossbow and hand gonnes…wherefore be it ordained and enacted by authority of this present Parliament that no person from henceforth shoot in any crossbow or any hand gonne … unless he …have land and tenents to the yearly value of 300 Marks.

(6 Hen. VIII c. 13)

9. HENRY RETREATS: 1523 - 1557

Henry VIII's policy against shooting of firearms proved one of the great disasters of his reign. In 1523, admitting that the law was widely disobeyed, Henry reduced the property qualification from lands worth 300 marks to lands worth 100 marks. (14 Hen. VIII c. 7). In 1539, with another French war on the horizon, Henry repealed the gun law entirely. (P. Hughes & J. Larkin, Tudor Royal Proclamations, Vol.1 at 372 (1969)). By 1540, guns were so popular that Henry complained that his subjects were target shooting inside cities and towns," without any regard or respect for where their pellets do fall or light down after their shot," so that "sundry his Grace's officers and subjects, being on the highway, in the open street, or in their own houses, chambers or gardens, have been put in great jeopardy...." (P. Hughes & J. Larkin, Tudor Royal Proclamations, Vol.1 at 372 (1969)). The following year, Henry reapplied his gun ban, although narrowing it to apply only to certain firearms with relatively short barrels, and expressly provided that any inhabitant of a city might own longer firearms and practice with them (on target butts only; Henry was not forgetting the experiences of the previous year!). (33 Hen. VIII c.6). Five years later, acknowledging "how expedient it was to have his loving subjects practiced and exercised in the feat of shooting of handguns" Henry had to remind his subjects that they were expected to conform to the renewed law. (Hughes & Larkin, supra, at 372). At length, Henry gave up and repealed the entire gun law by proclamation. (N. Perrin, Giving up the Gun 62 (1978)).

10. PHILLIP AND MARY ENACT THE FIRST MILITIA STATUTE: 1557

By the end of Henry's reign, it was obvious that the days of the longbow were numbered and that firearms would dominate the military future. It was also obvious that increased organization and drilling was needed. Thus in 1557 Henry's daughter Mary proclaimed what may be considered the first of the true militia statutes (the word 'militia'was not actually applied to persons subject to it for another thirty years). Its length and complexity (it occupies four large pages of fine print in the statute books, and apportions weapon requirements by no fewer than eighteen classes of property) precludes giving more than a few selections here. While bows were still required of some persons, firearms (listed as haquebutts, today spelled arquebus, an early form of shoulder firearm) are also listed.

> For the better furniture and defense of this Realme, be it enacted....
>
> All and every person temporal having (lands) to the clear yearly value of one thousand pounds or above shall...have,find, keep and maintain...six horses or geldings suitable for demilances (light armored cavalry)...and ten light horses or geldings suitable and meet for light horsemen, with the furniture and harness and weapons requisite for the same...and also forty corselettes furnished, ...forty pikes, thirty long bows, thirty sheafes of arrows, ...twenty haquebutts....
>
> And (every person) having goods and chattels to the value of 200 pounds and above, and under 400 pounds, (shall have) one corselet furnished, one pike...one haquebutt, one murain or sallet (infantry helmet), two long bows, two sheafes of arrows, and two skulls or steel caps....

(4 & 5 Phil. & Mar. c. 2,3)

11. ELIZABETH RECEIVES REPORTS ON MILITIA MUSTERS AND PROMOTION OF SHOOTING

The Calendar of State Papers was compiled in the 19th century as a summary of the archives of previous reigns. The following selections from 1569 show how far the English had progressed toward universal firearm ownership even at this time—nearly forty years before the Jamestown settlement in the new world. They also reflect responses to a recent policy of the Privy Council aimed at increasing the number of persons using firearms—the arquebuses or harquebuses.

> July 2. Lord North and others, Commissioners of Musters for the County of Cambridge, to the Council. Certifying their doings in the musters. Enclosing, a certificate of the musters for the

County of Cambridge....

July 3. The Dean of York (and others) to Sir William Cecil. Have taken musters of armor etc. of the clergy within the Diocese of York, and transmit a schedule of the same....

July 10. ...Commission of Musters for Surrey to the Council. Give their opinions and answers to the various articles sent to them from the Council, relative to the increase of harquebusiers within that County....

Sir William Wygston, Sir Thomas Lucy, and others, Commissioners of Musters for the County of Warwick, to the Council. Reply to their letters as to the increase of harquebusiers in that county. Have appointed diverse places for the practice of shooting....

Earl of Huntingdon, Sir Thomas Nevell, and others, Commissioners of Muster for the County of Leicester, to the Council. Certify their doings in the musters. Desire a longer time for exercising their men in the caliver (a smaller caliber and more modern form of arquebus).

Lord Cobham, Sir Thomas Kemp, and others, Commissioners of Musters for the County of Kent, to the Council. Report their opinion concerning the increase of harquebusiers in that county ...estimate the expense of establishing certain places for the practice of harquebusiers in the County of Kent, and of rewards of those who shall be skillful in shooting with the harquebus.

(Calendar of State Papers (Domestic) Elizabeth I, Vol. 54, at 338-40)

12. A TUDOR HISTORIAN PRAISES ARMAMENT OF ALL CITIZENS AS AN ENGLISH VIRTUE: 1476

The association between arms ownership and the English way of life did not pass unnoticed even in the 15th century. Sir John Fortescue is believed to have been born in 1394. After serving as Chief Justice of King's Bench, he wrote his Governance of England sometime around 1476. It is generally considered the first English political writing founded upon experience rather than theory or theology. Fortescue's thesis was that England had developed a limited monarchy, a monarchy under law, while France had developed an absolutist monarchy. Quite a sophisticated theme for the 15th century! In order to retain the flavor of the original, the original spelling is first given below, followed by a modernized 'translation'.

> Thai gon crokyd, and ben feble, not able to fight, nor to defend the realm; nor thai haue wepen, nor money to bie thaim wepen withall. But verely thai liuen in the most extreme pouertie and miserie, and yet dwellyn thai in on the most fertile reaume of the worlde. Werthurgh the French kynge hath not men of his owne reaume able to defende it, except his nobles, wich beyren non such imposicions, and ther fore thai ben right likely of thair bodies; bi wich cause the said kynge is compellid to make his armeys and retinues for the defence of his lande of straungers, as Scottes, Spaynardes, Arrogoners, men of Almeyn, and of other nacions, or ellis all his enymes myght ouerrenne hym; for he hath no defence of his owne except his castels and fortresses. Lo, this is the fruit of jus reale. Yf the reaume of Englonde, wich is an Ile, and therfor mey not lyghtly geyte succore of other landes, were rulid under such a lawe, and under such a prince, it wolde be than a pray to all other nacions that wolde conqwer, robbe or deuouir it....
>
> They (the french peasants) grow crooked, and become feeble, not able to fight nor to defend the realm; nor do they have weapons, nor the money to buy them weapons withal. But truly they live in the most extreme poverty and misery, and yet dwell in the most fertile realm of the world. Wherefore the French king hath not men of his own realm to defend it, except the nobles, which bear not such impositions, and therefore are very cautious of risking their bodies; by which cause the said king is compelled to make his armies and retinues for the defense of his land of strangers, as Scots, Spaniards, Arrogoners, men of Almeyn (Germany), and of other nations, or else his enemies might overrun him; for he hath no defense of his own except his castles and fortresses. If the realm of England, which is an isle, and therefore not likely to get aid of other realms, were ruled under such a law, and under such a prince, it would be a prey to all other nations that would conquer, rob, or devour it....

(Sir John Fortescue, The Governance of England: The Difference between an Absolute and a Limited Monarchy 114-15 (Rev. ed. 1885))

Thus by the beginning of the 17th century Englishmen had been accustomed for generations to a political-military system in which virtually every male, free or unfree, had arms and was trained in their use—indeed, in which a failure to be armed was a punishable dereliction of civic duty. The place of longbow had been taken by the firearm as Englishmen who had bought guns even when prohibited were now encouraged by militia statutes and government prizes. Alongside this had grown the concept that the arming of all citizens was a particularly English virtue—the key to their independence and individualism. It is not hard to predict the reaction engendered when, in the second half of the 17th century, English governments attempted to disarm their subjects.

THE CRUCIAL HALF-CENTURY:
1639 - 1689

"The right of his Majesty's protestant subjects to have arms for their own defense, and to use them for lawful purposes, is most clear and undeniable. It seems, indeed, to be considered, by the ancient laws of this kingdom, not only as a right, but as a duty."

A person interested in the background of the American constitution and Bill of Rights will find no period of English history more vital than the short span of 1639 to 1689. This half-century is a key—more properly, the key—to what a colonist of 1776 or an American of 1789 understood as his rights. In 1639, the English crown was worn by Charles I, who saw nothing wrong in informing Parliament that "I owe the account of my actions to God alone," or in imprisoning legislators who criticized him. Half a century later, the king and queen held power by grant of Parliament— an offer made only after they publicly swore to uphold a Declaration of Rights limiting their powers and defining the rights of their subjects. The change did not come easily. This relatively short period saw a prolonged civil war, a 'Glorious Revolution,' and a military dictatorship: of the three

Kings who then reigned, one was executed, another raised in exile, and the third driven from the country. The three turning points of the time were forever tied to these three kings: first, the civil war and establishment of a commonwealth under Cromwell; second, the restoration of the monarchy with Charles II; and third, the 'Glorious Revolution' and the Declaration of Rights.

"BY GOD, NOT FOR AN HOUR!": THE ENGLISH CIVIL WAR

At the death of Elizabeth in 1603, the English throne passed to the house of Stuart, represented by James I. Peace-loving to the point of obsession, he allowed repeal of the militia statute of Phillip and Mary. His son, Charles I, was forced in later years to try to restructure the militia by proclamation, without a specific statute. His plans would have involved training of virtually every adult male by instructors detailed from his small regular army—a plan he called the 'Exact Militia' (L. Boynton, The Elizabethan Militia 240 (1967)). Charles' financial needs led, however, to a confrontation with Parliament in 1639. Over the following three years Charles agreed to a variety of compromises, even to the execution of his best minister. Then Parliament demanded control of the militia. "By God, not for an hour!" exploded Charles. "You have asked that of me in this which was never asked of a King!" Charles tried to arrest five parliamentary leaders for treason, failed, and fled London to begin raising an army. Parliament did the same. A civil war between king and legislature had begun.

With the militia so largely decayed, both sides found it difficult to raise and arm troops. Their desperation led to measures ranging from disarming opponents to 'borrowing' the weapons of neutrals and allies felt unreliable. The result has been summarized by a modern historian: "Forewarned was forearmed, and from 1642 Englishmen learned to hide their firearms and to stockpile weapons." (J. Malcolm, 10 Hast. Con. L.Q. 285, 294).

13. CHARLES I COMPLAINS OF PARLIAMENTARY ARMS SEIZURES

One of Parliament's first moves was to enact a Militia Ordinance, seeking to control as many militia units as it could and, where it could not,to seize the county armories where militiamen sometimes stored their ammunition and spare arms.

> HIS MAJESTIES' ANSWER TO A PRINTED
> PAPER, INTITLED, A NEW DECLARATION
> OF THE LORDS AND COMMONS IN
> PARLIAMENT, OF THE 21st OF
> JUNE 1642
> We have always and do now declare, that the pretended or-
> dinances (of Parliament) against the law of the land, against the
> liberty and property of the subject...that we are bound by our oath
> (and all our Subjects are bound by theirs of allegience and
> Supremacy) to oppose that Ordinance which is already put in ex-
> ecution against us, not only by training and arming our subjects,
> but by forceably removing the magazines from the places trusted
> by the counties, to their own houses, and guarding it there with
> armed men; whither it will next be removed and how much used
> by such persons we know not.

(An Exact Collection of all Remonstrances, Declarations...and Othe₁ Remarkable Passages between the King's Most Excellent Majesty and his High Court of Parliament, at 380 (London, 1643))

14. A PARLIAMENTARY LEADER COMPLAINS OF CHARLES' ARMS SEIZURES

Charles protested too much. As Lilburn's great pamphlet argued, his supporters were hardly blameless.

> The militia of the County of Dunham was entrusted with Sir
> Henry Vane the elder...and Sir Henry Vane, having arms of his
> own in his house at Ruby Castle, sufficient to arm one hundred
> men, those arms were carried by his two principal lieutenants...to
> the town of Newcastle, where they were delivered to one ap-
> pointed by the Earl of Newscastle to receive them...all which be-

ing known in the county, the people were much disheartened, and for that the party entrusted with the militia had furnished the enemy as aforesaid, many were forced to take up arms under the command of the Earl of Newcastle, divrs for fear fled out of the county.

(John Lilburne, England's Birthright Justified, at 19 (London, 1645))

15. PARLIAMENT AUTHORIZES SEARCHES FOR ARMS

Parliament wasted no time in seeking new sources of arms—simply confiscating them from potential enemies.

INSTRUCTIONS FOR THE LORDS
LIEUTENANTS, COMMITTEES OF
PARLIAMENT, AND OTHER
OFFICERS AND COMMANDERS
...Fifthly, that the Lords Lieutenant and Committees...shall and may from time to time raise such and so many of the Trained Bands (organized militia), and other persons inhabiting in the said Cities and Counties, as they shall judge necessary and fitting, to enter into the Houses of all Papists, and other persons who are voted to be Delinquents by both or either of the Houses of Parliament...or that have been present with or aiding His Majesty...or such Clergymen and others that have publicly preached or declared themselves to oppose, disgrace or revile the proceedings of both or either Houses of Parliament; and to seize upon the Arms, Ammunition and Horses fit for Service in the War, that belong to such person....

(Ordinance of 9 January 1642, Ordinances and Acts of the Commonwealth and Protectorate, at 57)

16. PARLIAMENT ADOPTS ARMS REGISTRATION AND DISARMS THE OPPOSITION

Parliament won the first round of the civil war in 1646, when Charles fell into its hands. After renewed fighting in 1648 led to another victory,

Charles was executed. Parliament then proposed to demobilize its 'New Model Army', led by Oliver Cromwell. Since Parliament did not bother with a minor detail—the Army's pay was in arears for many months— the military reacted rather negatively. The army marched on London and took over the government. Over the next nine years, England went through a variety of governments as Cromwell and the army made and unmade new Parliaments. Cromwell's death in 1658 brought on another crisis.

AN ACT FOR SETTLING THE MILITIA IN ENGLAND AND WALES

...Be it further enacted by the Authority aforesaid, That all and every such Householder (within London)...shall on or before the Seven and Twentieth Day of July, 1659, deliver or cause to be delivered to such person or persons as shall be by this Act appointed to receive the same, a perfect and exact list of all Arms and Ammunition...in the possession of or belonging to such Householder and Lodger...

And for the better securing the Peace of the Commonwealth, Be it further Enacted and Ordained, that the said Commissioners or any three or more of them are hereby Enabled and Authorized from time to time, by Warrant under their Hands and Seals, to imploy such well-affected person or persons as they shall think fit...in the day time to search for, and seize all arms, in the Custody and Possession of any Popish Recusant, or other person that hath been in arms against the Parliament, or that have adhered to the enemies thereof, or any other person whom the Commissioners shall judge dangerous to the Peace of this Commonwealth, and with such Arms to Arm such well-affected persons as they shall think fit, or otherwise to secure such Arms for the use of the Commonwealth.

(Ordinances of 22 and 26 July 1659, Ordinances and Acts of the Commonwealth and Protectorate, at 1317, 1340)

RESTORATION AND DISARMAMENT: 1660

The Protectorate established by Cromwell did not long outlive him.

Within a year the remnants of the old Parliament were called and invited Charles II, the eldest son of the executed Charles I, to return from exile and take the throne. Neither Charles nor his parliaments wasted time consolidating their power. Charles disbanded all but a few loyal units of the army. Parliament essentially purged the Church of England of all but royalists; unlicensed preachers were forbidden to preach to groups of more than five persons or to come within five miles of any town where they had previously held services. Non-anglicans (Puritans, Catholics, Presbyterians and Anabaptists alike) were forbidden to hold political office. Cities which had sided with Parliament were subjected to direct royal control and their fortifications levelled.

17. CHARLES BEGINS DISARMING POSSIBLE OPPONENTS

Charles was hardly in power before orders were issued to the lords lieutenants of the militia, the chief militia officers of each county, to form units of royalist volunteers and disarm opponents. Soon, Charles established a system which parallelled that of the three-centuries later Gun Control Act of 1968.

> Gunsmiths were ordered to produce a record of all weapons they had manufactured over the past six months together with a list of their purchasers. In the future they were commanded to report every Saturday night to the ordinance office the number of guns made and sold that week. Carriers throughout the kingdom were required to obtain a license if they wished to transport guns, and all importation of firearms was banned.

(Malcolm, supra, at 299-300)

> July (1660). 188. Instructions issued to the Lords Lieutenants of the several counties, commanding the regular exercising of the troops, the full numbers to be kept up, well-affected officers chosen, the volunteers who offer assistance formed apart in troops and trained, the officers to be numerous, disaffected persons watched and not allowed to assemble, and their arms seized....

18. THE MILITIA ACT OF 1662: LEGAL POWER TO DISARM

Charles of course sought enactment of statutes giving him control over the militia and authorizing seizure of weapons. His initial efforts were defeated, largely due to resentment at the arms seizures and other harrassments of opponents. (J.R. Western, The English Militia in the Eighteenth Century 11 (1965)). After a year's efforts, he obtained only a general declaration that the king had the right to control the militia. (13 Car.II c. 6 (1661)). Only in 1662—after attacking the committee considering the bill and engaging in a major lobbying campaign—was Charles able to get a detailed militia statute enacted.

> Forasmuch as within all his Majesty's realms and dominions the sole and supreme power, government, command and disposition of the militia...is and by the laws of England ever was the undoubted right of his Majesty and his royal predecessors...be it therefore enacted...that the King's most excellent Majesty, his heirs and successors shall and may from time to time as occasion shall require issue forth several commissions of lieutenancy to such persons (as may be found fit), which lieutenants shall have full power and authority to call together all persons at such times and to arm and array them in such manner as is hereafter expressed....
>
> And for the better securing the peace of the Kingdom, be it further enacted and ordained, that the respective lieutenants or any two or more of their deputies are hereby enabled and authorized from time to time...to search for and seize all arms in the custody or possession of any person or persons whom the said lieutenants or any two or more of their deputies shall judge dangerous to the peace of the kingdom.

(14 Car. II c.3 (1662))

19. CHARLES EMPLOYS THE MILITIA ACT

Charles and his supporters wasted little time in using their power to seize arms under the Militia Act. Records of the time are filled with reports of mysterious plots by anti-royalists and 'nonconformists' (mostly puritans, Quakers and Anabaptists), and of seizures of their arms.

> Feb. 8 (1663). Sir John Norton and Sir J. Bennet, Deputy Lieutenants of Hampshire, to Lord Lieutenant the Earl of Southampton. Sends certain examinations; more eyes are needed where so many heads are at work. Think Fauntleroy an untoward fellow; arms for thirty or forty were found at his house last year ....
>
> March 22. Warrant to commit Jacob Knowles close prisoner to the gatehouse for dangerous designs, he having been taken on the guard, with a pistol upon him.
>
> Warrant to Simon Parry to search the houses of James Butler at Oatlands, and Major Dambrun at Weybridge, for arms, papers, and what else is suspicious....
>
> October 19. Warrant from Secretary Bennet to a messenger to seize the arms, books, papers, etc. of Rowerth, and bring him in safe custody....
>
> November 8. Wm. Nowell to Williamson. The deputy lieutenants of the city, hearing of a nonconformist meeting, issued warrants for search of arms; the officers being denied entrance, broke open the doors, and found two hundred or three hundred persons....
>
> November 9. J.F. to (the King). Has apprehended seven Quakers at a meeting six miles off, and sent them to Launceston goal; one, a gunsmith, confesses to fixing arms lately. Missed the speaker, who is a stranger, and frequents both Quakers and Anabaptists, enlisting men and arms.
>
> November 23. Sir William Bradshaigh to Williamson.... Has searched for arms, but with little success, for a general order of that effect being made, all but fools hide close....

(Calendar of State Papers (Domestic), Charles II, at 44, 83, 333, 346)

20. THE 1671 HUNTING ACT: DISARMAMENT OF ALL BUT MAJOR LANDOWNERS

In 1671, Parliament went still farther. Whereas the Militia Act had disarmed only individuals suspected of certain sympathies, the Hunting Act now broadly sought to disarm all persons not owning real estate worth 100 pounds annual rental. For several centuries England had possessed 'hunting acts' which barred hunting by the poor. Possession of certain hunting implements (nets, traps, hunting dogs, etc.) was likewise prohibited. The 1671 Act included firearms among the items which could not be possessed, and raised the qualification to ownership of land worth 100 pounds sterling rental value—fifty times the property requirement for voting! It also eliminated hunting and gun rights for those who, while not poor, owned little land, thus disarming merchants, mechanics, and others of the town-based middle class. The large landowners were, moreover, empowered to enforce the act themselves, and to search homes of other citizens in their area upon 'suspicion' of gun ownership.

> Whereas diverse disorderly persons, laying aside their lawful trades and employments do betake themselves to the stealing, taking and killing of conies (rabbits), hares, pheasants, partridges and other game, intended reserved by former laws, with guns, dogs, trammels...be it enacted that all lords of manors...may take and seize all such guns, bows, greyhounds...or other dogs...as within the precincts of such respective manors shall be used by any person or persons who are by this act prohibited to keep the same; and moreover...may in the daytime search the houses, out-houses, or other places of any such person or persons prohibited by this act to keep the same, as upon good ground shall be suspected to have or keep in his custody any guns, bows, greyhounds (etc.)....
>
> And it is hereby enacted and declared, that all and every person and persons not having lands...of the clear yearly value of 100 pounds per annum...are hereby declared by the laws of this realm not allowed to have or keep for themselves, or any other person or persons, any guns, bows, greyhounds...but shall be and are hereby prohibited to have, keep or use the same.

(22-23 Car. II c.25)

21. JAMES II CONTINUES THE ARMS SEIZURES BEGUN BY CHARLES

Upon the death of Charles, his brother, James II, succeeded to the throne. James continued Charles' approach, but did so with two handicaps. First, he was obvious and frank about his intentions; second, he was a Catholic, the last such to sit upon the English throne. What had been acceptable tactics for Charles became evidences of oppression under James.

December 6 (1686). The Earl of Sutherland to the Earl of Burlington. The king having received information that a great many persons not qualified by law, under pretence of shooting matches, keep muskets or other guns in their houses, it is his pleasure that you should send orders to your deputy lieutenants to cause strict search to be made for such muskets or guns and to seize and safely keep them until further order. Memorandum: like letters sent to (the other lords lieutenant).

March 10 (1687). The Earl of Middleton to any of the messengers or to John Dawndle. Warrant to search the house of Robert Sanders...against whom information of suspicious and dangerous practices tending to disturb the public peace has been given, and if they find there any arms of armor of any new form or fashion such as for number or quality becomes not one of his condition to have, to seize him and them and to bring them before the Earl to be dealt with as the law shall direct.

November 2. Warrant to James Kitson, messenger. Information having been given of a great number of carabines, pistols and other arms, concealed in a certain house in or near the city of London, whereof you shall have notice, these are in his Majesty's name, to authorize and require you forthwith to repair to the said house...and search for all such arms as are concealed....

(Calendar of State Papers (Domestic), James II, Vol. 2 at 314, Vol. 3 at 95)

22. JAMES EXTENDS THE CONFISCATIONS TO IRELAND

By James' time, England had established military control of Ireland and begun settling colonists there. Although the relationship between the nations was not so bad as it would be following the oppressive laws enacted by James' successor, resentment for the colonists often flared into violence. When James' disarmament policies were extended to the colonists, James' opponents feared he meant to sacrifice them. As a later critic of James wrote: "Already the designs of the Court began gradually to unfold themselves. A royal order came...for disarming the population. This order (James' General) Tyrconnel strictly executed as respected the English. Though the country was infested by predatory bands, a protestant gentleman could scarcely obtain permission to keep a brace of pistols." (T. Macaulay, The History of England, vol. 2 at 137 (11th ed. 1856)). In the following passage, the Earl of Clarendon, Lord Lieutenant for Ireland, gives a more sympathetic view.

> January 19. Dublin Castle. ...On Sunday last I had several accounts brought to me of great insolences committed by the Tories (bandits) in the county of Cork, and of great robberies in that county and in Limerick, that many people were set upon in the daytime and dangerously wounded. ... One of these informations seeming to impute much of the unruliness of the Tories to the English being disarmed, I thought fit to take that occasion to acquaint the Lords of the Council here with the power the King gives me by his letter of the 30th of November last to dispense with the execution of the 29th article of my instruction... it is a thing of great importance what persons should be trusted with arms and ought to be very well considered before any are delivered out.

(Calendar of State Papers (Domestic), James II, Vol. 2 at 314, Vol. 3 at 95)

AN ABOMINABLE THING, TO DISARM THE NATION": THE GLORIOUS REVOLUTION AND THE DECLARATION OF RIGHTS.

James' reign was brief. He was speedily overthrown when his son-in-law and daughter, William and Mary, nominally 'invaded' England. English political and military leaders defected to William and Mary en masse. James fled to France. From first to last, the 'Glorious Revolution' of 1688 cost not one life.

The Revolution left a major question unanswered. James had, after all, been crowned king and was still very much alive. His daughter Mary could hardly claim a right to the throne—much less her husband. The conservative royalists, whose support had been vital to the Revolution, were willing to unseat James as a threat to their church and property, but were unwilling to agree that Parliament had a right to 'appoint' a new king.

The solution was finally found. Parliament (in the absence of a king, calling itself a 'convention' ruling upon 'declarations') ruled that James, by fleeing England, had voluntarily given up the throne. But Parliament was unwilling to risk substituting one absolute monarch for another. It proceeded to pass a 'Declaration of Rights', defining the basic rights of Englishmen, including a clearly individual right to keep and bear arms. Before assuming the throne, William and Mary were required to swear to uphold these rights; their first parliament then enacted the guarantee as the "Bill of Rights".

To a modern mind, the events of 1688 are obscure. Of those who study or expound upon the American Bill of Rights, it is doubtful that one in a hundred realizes that many of its guarantees were taken (some word-for-word) from another Bill of Rights a century before. The founders of our own nation were not so forgetful. 1688 was to them a high-water mark of freedom, an obvious predecessor to their own age. The similarity between the 1688 Declaration of Rights and our own Bill of Rights is no coincidence: no founder of our own nation would have claimed fewer rights than those allowed an Englishman of a century before.

23. THE HOUSE OF COMMONS DRAFTS A DECLARATION OF RIGHTS

The House committee charged with drafting a Declaration of Rights initially reported out a version which, while providing that all seized arms be returned, spoke in terms that stressed public duty rather than an individual right.

> It is the right of the subjects to petition the King: and that all such committments and prosecutions for such petitions are illegal.
> The Acts concerning the Militia are grievous to the subject.
> It is necessary for the public safety, that the subjects, which are protestants, should provide and keep arms for their common

defense; and that the arms which have been seized and taken from them be restored.

(Journal of the House of Commons from Dec. 26, 1688 to Oct. 26, 1693, at 17 (London, 1742))

24. COMMONS, DEBATING THE DECLARATION, COMPLAINS OF GUN SEIZURES

Since seventeenth-century legislative records are sparse, we are fortunate that Lord Somers, who chaired the drafting committee, saved his pencilled notes of the floor debates, which notes were years later obtained and published by Attorney General Phillip Hardwicke. These notes show that the seizures of arms under the Militia Act figured prominently in the debates and that the members of the House of Commons, some of whom had themselves been the victims, intended to ensure against these in the future.

Notes of what passed in the Convention upon the day the question was moved in the House of Commons concerning the abdication of King James II, the 20th of January 1688.

Mr. Dolben. Vacancy in the government, and the King demise. The King withdrawn without provision—fact clear, law plain. ...moves, that it is the opinion of the committee, that King James II is demised, by voluntary departure, in consequence of which the government is without a king....

Sergeant Maynard:.... The true question is, whether the King has not deposed himself? Put the case and it will appear to no one—all mixed government has its foundation in consent—it is clear there may be transgressions, as will not amount to a forfeiture, but will prove to all that he ought to govern no longer. ... An Act of Parliament was made to disarm all Englishmen, whom the lieutenant should suspect, by day or by night, by force or by otherwise—this was done in Ireland for the sake of putting arms into Irish hands....

Sir William Williams. Settled the terms—would enact no new constitution, but make declaration only and pursue the old. ...

Mr. Christy. A Magna Carta—a coronation oath to preserve

the protestant religion.

Sir Richard Temple. Not launch into such a sea—three heads (headings); first, provide against encroaching on parliaments for posterity...second, standing armies settled without consent of Parliament, though no part of constitution—may be allowed in case of war, invasion, or rebellion—Militia Bill—power to disarm all Englishmen—now done in Ireland—Third, Westminister Hall must be better filled, with persons who are honest....

Mr. Boscawen. Arbitrary power exercised by the ministry (government)—militia—imprisoning without reason; disarming, himself disarmed....

Sergeant Maynard. ...—some gross grievances for which we are beholden to a Parliament who cared not what was done, so their pensions (salaries) were paid—Militia Act—an abominable thing to disarm the nation, and set up a standing army.

(Phillip Hardwicke, Miscellaneous State Papers From 1501 to 1726, Vol. 2 at 401-17 (London, 1778))

25. THE HOUSE OF LORDS PROPOSES A CLEARLY INDIVIDUAL RIGHT TO ARMS

In the Lords, the portion of the Declaration dealing with arms was amended in a way that clearly guaranteed the right of most Englishmen, as individuals, to own arms. Indeed, the omission of militia concerns in the final draft has attracted attention from military historians who feel the needs of the militia were ignored. "The original wording implied that everyone had a duty to be ready to appear in arms whenever the state was threatened. The revised wording suggested only that it was lawful to keep a blunderbus to repel burglars." (J.R. Western, Monarchy and Revolution 339 (1972)). The Lords version prevailed in conference, and became the Declaration and later Bill of Rights.

And thereupon the said Lords Spiritual and Temporal and Commons...do in the first place (as their ancestors in like case have usually done) for the vindicating and asserting their ancient rights and liberties declare:

...That it is the right of the subjects to petition the King, and all commitments and prosecutions for such petitioning are illegal;...that the subjects which are protestant may have arms for their defense suitable to their condition and as allowed by law.

(Journal of the House of Commons, supra, at 29 (London, 1742))

26. AN ENGLISH COURT RECOGNIZES LEGALITY OF GUN OWNERSHIP

Parliament did not hesitate to make it clear that the Bill of Rights was intended to override prior statutes and establish a broad right of arms ownership. It re-enacted the Game Act, omitting 'guns' from the list of items prohibited to those not allowed to hunt. (4 & 5 Wm. & Mary c.23; 5 Ann. c.14). Thereafter, English courts, grand juries, and legal writers stressed that possession of firearms was entirely lawful. (See generally Malcolm, supra, at 310-13.) In Wingfield, a defendant had been convicted of a Game Act violation and his gun was confiscated upon a claim that it was an 'engine'(device) for poaching, and since the Game Act permitted seizure of such 'engines,' could be confiscated. The court refused to allow the forfeiture, holding that the prosecutor had failed to allege that the gun had actually been used to break the law—simple possession by a person not entitled to hunt was not enough.

> It is not to be imagined that it was the intention of the legislature, in making the 5 Ann c.14 to disarm all the people of England. As (hunting dogs, traps, etc.) are expressly mentioned in that statute, it is never necessary to alledge, that any of these have been used for killing or destroying the game.... But as Guns are not expressly mentioned in that statute, and as a Gun may be kept for the defense of a man's House, and for divers other lawful purposes, it was necessary to alledge, in order to its being comprehended within the meaning of the words 'any other Engines to kill the Game', that the Gun had been used for killing the Game.

(Wingfield v. Stratford, 96 Eng. Rep. 787 (King's Bench 1752))

27. AN ENGLISH LEGAL OFFICIAL CONSTRUES THE DECLARATION OF RIGHTS

The Declaration of Rights and accompanying statutes became known as the 'Revolution Settlement', which was seen as the core of the British unwritten constitution. To the statesmen and writers of the 1700's, "the year 1689 seemed the last year of creation, when God looked upon England and saw that it was good." (G.M. Trevelyan, The English Revolution 8 (1979)). When the Recorder of London, chief legal official for that City, was asked for an opinion on the legality of a proposal to privately embody a group for training in the use of arms, it was natural that he resort to the 1688 Declaration. It is interesting that the Recorder counseled essentially that the association's right to arm and train for civil purposes was unquestionable, but that it should not claim to do so for military purposes, even with a Royal commission, since such commissions might be of dubious legality without Parliamentary approval.

> It is a matter of some difficulty to define the precise limits and extent of the rights of the people of this realm to bear arms, and to instruct themselves in the use of them, collectively; and much more so to point out all the acts of that kind, which would be illegal or doubtful in their nature.
>
> The right of his Majesty's protestant subjects to have arms for their own defense, and to use them for lawful purposes, is most clear and undeniable. It seems, indeed, to be considered, by the ancient laws of this kingdom, not only as a right, but as a duty. …And that this right which every protestant most unquestionable possesses individually may, and in many cases must, be exercised collectively, is likewise a point which I conceive to be most clearly established.…
>
> (I)t seems to follow, of necessary consequence, that it cannot be unlawful to learn to use them (for such lawful purposes) with safety and effect. For it would be too gross an absurdity to allege, that it is not lawful to be instructed in the use of anything which is lawful to use.…
>
> The lawful purposes for which such arms may be used (besides immediate self-defense) are the suppression of violent and felonious breaches of the peace, the assistance of the civil magistrates in the execution of the laws, and the defense of the kingdom against foreign invaders.… in any other situation but that of invasion by a foreign enemy, I should very much doubt not only

the propriety, but the legality, of any commissions granted by the crown to armed associations not previously voted by Parliament.

To apply these principles to the case of the London Association: I can see nothing in their plan or conduct which can justly be considered a violation of the laws....

To strengthen the civil power, and to keep themselves at all times prepared for a vigorous and effectual discharge of their duty as citizens...are, in my view, sufficient visible and legal objects for the continuation of the association....I would recommend it to this respectable body, to consider themselves a civil, and not a military, association, and confine themselves, in the present state of things, to those civil objects which will, upon the principles laid down, sufficiently justify them in exercising and perfecting themselves in the use of arms, without any commission whatever.

(W. Blizzard, Desultory Reflections on Police (London, 1785))

AN ARMED PEOPLE: PROLOGUE TO REVOLUTION

"Were our militia well regulated, and firearms substituted in place of bows...we'd need not fear a hundred thousand enemies.... The preservation of the game is but a very slender excuse for omitting it. I hope no wise man will put a hare or a partridge in balance with the safeties and liberties of...men."

In the American colonies, there was no need to debate the ownership of arms as a right: it had long since become a fact of life. Two factors underscored the importance of arms bearing. The first factor was the colonial militia statutes which, in light of immediate threats from Indians, French, Dutch and Spaniards, maintained the requirement that virtually all males be armed and trained. The second was an intellectual factor—the development of the Whig political philosophy and its almost universal acceptance in the colonies.

UNIVERSAL GUN OWNERSHIP AS A LEGAL DUTY: THE COLONIAL MILITIA LAWS

28. NEW PLYMOUTH COLONY

The militia laws of New Plymouth colony, which was later incorporated into Massachusetts, are typical of the early American statutes. It is interesting that the colony was requiring stockpiling of flintlocks (snaphaunces or 'firelocks') as early as 1646, when such weapons were expensive novelties in England itself. By 1677, when the British army was still using matchlocks, ownership of flintlocks was mandatory for civilians in the colony.

> (1632 Session) In regard toward dispersions so far assunder and the inconvenience may befall, it is further ordered that every freeman or other inhabitant of this colony provide for himself and each under him able to bear arms a sufficient musket and serviceable peece for war with bandeleros (ammunition bandolier) and…he be at all times after the last of May next ensuing furnished with two pounds of powder and ten pounds of bullets, and for each default in himself or servant to forfeit ten shillings.
>
> (1640) That the inhabitants of every towne within the government fitt and able to bear arms be trained at least six times in the year.
>
> (1646) …before the next October Court, each township shall provide two sufficient snaphaums (snaphaunces) or firelock pieces, two swords and two pouches for every thirty men they have in their township….
>
> (1677) It is enacted by this Court….that all persons required by the laws of this colony to keep and maintain arms be at all times provided with suffient fixt (operational) feirlocks or snaphance muskets or other serviceable peces not exceeding four foot and a half long nor under coliver bore (about .50 caliber) on penalty of six shillings…It is enacted by this Court that … the military commission officers of this jurisdiction…not only train their soldiers in their postures and motions, but also in shooting at markes (targets)….

(William Brigham, The Compact with the Charter and Laws of the Colony of New Plymouth, at 31, 84, 184 (Boston, 1836))

29. VIRGINIA LAWS OF ARMS BEARING

The Virginia colony, which was settled before its New England counterparts,had an earlier start on militia statutes.

> (1623) That no man go or send abroad without a sufficient party well armed. That men not go to work in the ground without their arms and a centinell (sentinel) upon them…that the commander of every plantation take care there be sufficient of powder and ammunition within the plantation under his command and their pieces fixt and their arms complete.
>
> (1631) No men shall go to work in the grounds without their arms, and a centinell upon them. All men that are fitting to bear arms, shall bring their pieces to the church….

(William Hening, The Statutes at Large, being a Collection of all the Laws of Virginia, Vol. 1 at 127, 173-74 (1823))

30. MILITIA LAWS OF THE COLONY OF NEW JERSEY

With the passage of time, simple legal commands to have or carry arms evolved into detailed militia statutes which required organization and military training. The following, a 1744 New Jersey enactment, illustrates the amount of arms, ammunition and training expected of the average colonist prior to the Revolution.

> 1. That after the publication of this Act, every Captain should make a true and perfect List of all the men within the District or Division of which he is Captain, between the age of seventeen and sixty, which he shall give to the Colonel….
>
> 2. That the Captain general or Commander in Chief may order one or two troops of Horse (cavalry) (as he shall deem it necessary) consisting of 50 men each, to be raised in each County….
>
> 3. Every person of a foot (infantry) company shall be armed

with a good musket or fusee (a short-barrelled musket),well fixed, and a bayonet fixed to it, a cutting sword or cutlace, a cartouche (cartridge) box or powder horn, with six charges of powder and six sizeable bullets at least, and shall appear at the time and place of muster so armed; and shall keep at his Place of Abode, beside what is above mentioned, one Pound of Powder and four Pounds of Bullets, and shall bring them into the field, if required. Each horseman shall be provided with a good horse, a Saddle, Breast Plate (armor)...holsters, a Case of Pistols, a cutting sword...and shall keep at the Place of his Abode, beside the Arms abovementioned, a well fix'd Carbine....

3.(sic) That the Colonel or Commanding Officer, in each County shall muster and exercise all the companies under his Command at least once a year....each Captain shall exercise his men four times a year....

(Wm. Whitehead, Documents Relating to the Colonial History of the State of New Jersey, Vol. 6 at 192-93 (1882))

THE WHIGS AND AMERICAN POLITICAL PERCEPTION

In terms of political thinking, no philosophy had as much influence on colonial Americans (or any other Americans, for that matter) as the writings of the English Whigs. The Whigs and their opponents the Tories had formed in the strife over the succession of James II to the throne. It is hard to define the exact principles of either party, but the Whigs essentially favored local over national government, the country gentry over members of the royal court, and parliament over king. It is hard to overstate the degree to which colonial Americans identified with the Whigs: John Adams estimated that fully nine-tenths of Americans were Whigs by the outbreak of the Revolution. (C. Rossiter, The Political Thought of the America Revolution 55 (1963)). Jefferson felt the Revolution itself mainly attributable to "the tory education of the king." (10 The Papers of Thomas Jefferson 369, 372 (1950)).The identification of 'American Patriot' with 'Whig' survives in a modified form to this day—Americans still commonly use 'Tory' to designate those who sided with the British government. The Whigs whose writings follow were studied carefully by Jefferson, Madison, Adams, form essentially the core political thought of the colonial period. (See H. Trevor Colburn, The Lamp of Experience: Whig History and the Intellectual Origins of the American Revolution 211, 218-25 (1965)).

31. RALEIGH ON THE BASES OF TYRANNY

To be sure, Sir Walter Raleigh cannot be classed as a 'Whig': he died decades before that term was invented. At the same time, his writings were standard references for any Whig and could be found in many public libraries, as well as in those of Jefferson and Madison (Colbourn, supra; R. Rutland, Madison's Bookish Habits (1980)). In the first portion of the following, Raleigh borrows heavily from Machiavelli; in the second he lists maxims of obvious and of subtle tyrants.

> Among the other dangers which a prince incurreth by being disarmed, is that thereby he becometh contemptible; for no comparison there is between he that is armed and they that are disarmed; and no reason there is that he that is armed should yield obedience to him that is disarmed....
> MAXIMS OF STATE:
> Sophisms of a barbarous and professed tyranny:....
> 2. To make sure to him and his state his military men by reward, liberty and other means....
> 3. To unarm his people of weapons, money and all things whereby they may resist his powers....
> Sophisms of the Sophistical or Subtle Tyrant, to hold up his State:....
> 8. To unarm his people, and store up their weapons, under pretence of keeping them safe, and having them ready when service requireth, and then to arm ...such as he shall think sure men....
> These rules of hypocritical tyrants are to be known, that they may be avoided, and met withal, and not drawn into imitation.

(The Works of Sir Walter Raleigh,Knight, Vol. 8 at 22, 25 (Oxford Univ. 1829))

32. MOLESWORTH CALLS FOR A MILITIA AND UNIVERSAL ARMAMENT

Roger Molesworth was one of the earliest of the Whig writers; his Franco-Gallia was in fact a translation of a work by a French scholar, which argued that most European governments had been republics in their earliest form—so that kings were not so 'by right of God,' but by recent usurpation of the rights of their citizens. Molesworth's writings were to be found in the libraries of Jefferson and John Adams, as well as a number of colonial public libraries. (Colbourne, supra). In the section which follows, Molesworth's introduction sets forth his "notion of a Whig, I mean a real Whig":

> A Whig is against the raising or keeping up a standing army in time of peace.... And therefore the arming and training of all the freeholders (landowners) of England, as is our undoubted ancient constitution, and consequently is our right; so it is the opinion of most Whigs, that it ought to be put into practice.... Were our militia well regulated, and firearms substituted in the place of bows, bill and arrows (the weapons in use when our training laws were in their vigor, and for which our laws are yet enforced) we'd need not fear a hundred thousand enemies, were it possible to land so many among us.... That this is not only practicable but easy, the modern example of the Swissers and Swedes is an undeniable indication.... The preservation of the game is but a very slender excuse for omitting it. I hope no wise man will put a hare or a partridge in balance with the safeties and liberties of Englishmen....

(Roger Molesworth, Introduction, Franco-Gallia, xxviii (London, 1721))

33. JAMES HARRINGTON SUPPORTS AN ARMED PEOPLE

Harrington was among the first Whigs to create a theory of political systems. Harrington's Oceana was his Utopia; The Prerogative of Popular Government was his defense of Oceana against critics. Harrington's writings were to be found in the Harvard library as well as many public and private libraries throughout the colonies. John Adams, whose thought was profoundly influenced by Harrington, obtained two sets of his writings for his library; Benjamin Rush, William Byrd and other colonists had to be content with one. (Colbourn, supra, at 210-15).

> For the government of citizens, as it is of two kinds, an equal or an unequal commonwealth, the reasons why it is the hardest to be conquered are also of two kinds; as first, the reasons why a government of citizens, where the commonwealth is equal, is hardest to be conquered is that the invader of such a society must not only trust unto his own strength, inasmuch as, the commonwealth being equal, he must needs find them united, but in regard that such citizens, being all soldiers or trained up unto their arms, which they use not for the defence of slavery but of liberty (a condition not in this world to be bettered) they have more especially on this occasion the highest soul of courage and (if their territory be of any extent) the vastest body of a well disciplined militia that is possible in nature. Wherefore, an example of such a one overcome by the arms of a monarch, is not to be found in the world....
>
> The reasons why a government of citizens, where the commonwealth is unequal, is next the former the hardest to be conquered are the same, with this difference, that albeit her peace is not perfect within, her condition is not to be bettered by anything without. Wherefore Rome in all her strife never called in an enemy....
>
> To conclude this part, for the reasons why a government of citizens...is the hardest to be held (in subjugation) there needs no more than that men accustomed to their arms and their liberties will never endure the yoke.

(James Harrington, Oceana and The Prerogative of Popular Government (1656; reprinted 1737))

34. ANDREW FLETCHER PRAISES AN ARMED CITIZENRY

Andrew Fletcher, another early Whig who enjoyed wide readership in the colonies, gave still greater stress to the concept of the armed citizenry.

> The subjects formerly had a real security for their liberty, by having the sword in their own hands. That security, which is the

greatest of all others, is lost, and not only so, but the sword is put into the hand of the King by his power over the Militia. All this is not enough; but we must have in both kingdoms standing armies of mercenaries....

For though as to other things, the constitution be ever so slight, a good militia will always preserve the public security. But in the best constitution that ever was, as to all other parts of government, if the militia be not upon a right foot, the liberty of the people must perish. The militia of ancient Rome, the best that ever was in any government, made her mistress of the world; but standing armies enslaved that great people and their excellent militia and freedom perished together. The Lacedomians continued eight hundred years free, and in good honor, because they had a good militia. The Swiss at this day are the freest, happiest, and the people of all Europe who can best defend themselves, because they have the best militia....

And I cannot see, why arms should be denied to any man who is not a slave, since they are the only true badges of liberty; and ought not ever, but in times of utmost necessity, to be put in the hands of mercenaries or slaves; neither can I understand why any man that has arms, should not be taught the use of them.

(Andrew Fletcher, A Discourse of Government with Relation to Militias (1737))

35. JAMES BURGH, WRITING ON THE EVE OF OUR REVOLUTION, PRAISES THE RIGHT TO BEAR ARMS

If Whiggism was the American political philosophy, James Burgh was the Whig as far as most colonists were concerned. Burgh corresponded with Jefferson, and enlisted Ben Franklin as editor for his Political Disquisitions. (Colbourn, supra, at 128). Copies of his first American edition were quickly bought by Washington, Jefferson, John Hancock, Oliver Dickinson and others; John Adams' copy was an autographed presentation from the author. (L. D. Cress, Citizens in Arms 35 (1982)). From the Whig standpoint, Political Disquisitions was indeed "the key book of the generation." (B. Bailyn, Ideological Origins of the American Revolution 41 (1977)). Writing as the Revolution was breaking out, Burgh attributed virtually all the colonists' grievances to the English substitution of a standing army for a militia, which relieved the royal court and tory ministry ('bureaucracy' is the closest modern equivalent) of fears of an 'armed people'.

> The confidence which a standing army gives a minister puts him upon carrying things with a higher hand, than he would attempt to do if the people were armed and the court unarmed, that is, if there were no land force in the nation, but a militia. Had we at this time no standing army, we would not think of forcing money out of the pockets of three millions of our (American) subjects. We would not think of punishing with military execution, unconvicted and unheard, our brave American children, our surest friends and best customers.... We would not think of making governors the needy and often worthless dependents of our corrupt court, by giving them power of appointing and removing judges.... We should not—but there is no end to observation of the differences between the measures likely to be pursued by a minister backed by a standing army, and those of a court awed by the fear of an armed people.

(James Burgh, Political Disquisitions, Vol. 2 at 341, 473, 476 (London 1775))

36. WILLIAM BLACKSTONE, TORY JURIST, PROCLAIMS THE WHIG VIEW OF ARMS BEARING

Common law legal training was long handicapped by the lack of any suitable reference works. No one set of writings was comprehensive, well organized, and readable. This changed when William Blackstone, an authoritative common law jurist, organized and published his lectures. The work became, not merely the most popular legal treatise of the age, but one of the most printed books of the century. Virtually every colonial lawyer, and every layman who desired a grasp of the law, began by studying Blackstone. (Too many also ended their study there: when St. George Tucker in 1803 brought out an edition of Blackstone annotated with American decisions, he commented in the introduction that many American lawyers were unaware of changes since the Revolution, relying on Blackstone to the exclusion of American decisions). Although Blackstone was a Tory, a great many of his views approached Whiggism: Whigs were more than happy to appropriate his description of their rights as rooted in history.

Blackstone's analysis of rights begins with 'absolute rights' under the common law, largely those of personal liberty and property. He then documents the 'auxiliary rights,' or political rights which safeguard the absolute rights. To Blackstone, these included the right to petition the King, to seek redress in court, constitutional limitations on royal power, and the right to have arms and use them in self defense.

> The fifth and last auxiliary right of the subject, that I shall at present mention, is that of having arms for their defense, suitable to their condition and degree and such as are allowed by law. Which is also declared by the same statute 1 W & M st.2 c.2 (the Bill of Rights) and it is indeed a public allowance under due restrictions, of the natural right of resistance and self-preservation, when the sanctions of society and the laws are found insufficient to restrain the violence of oppression. In these several articles consists the rights, or, as they are frequently termed, the liberties of Englishmen....

(Wm. Blackstone, Commentaries on the Law of England, Vol. 1 at 144 (1765))

To an American of the 18th century, firearms ownership was thus not only commonplace, but a civic duty. He lived—as had his ancestors for generations—under a legal obligation to own arms and be trained in their use. To the extent that he studied politics, history, or law, he encountered the unanimous opinion that individual ownership of arms was the sole security and distinction of a modern republic, and public disarmament the hallmark of tyranny. The emphasis put upon rights to keep and bear arms in the revolutionary period is thus not a matter of clumsy thinking or sloppily-drafted restrictions on standing armies. It was the natural response of men like James Madison, who served as a marksmanship instructor to the militia and felt that a tyranny could not be safe "without a standing army, an enslaved press, and a disarmed populace," or Thomas Jefferson, who advised his nephew "Let your gun therefore be the constant companion of your walks. Never think of taking a book with you," and sought to insert in the Virginia Constitution a guarantee that "No freeman shall ever be debarred the use of arms." (Madison autobiography, ms. collection, Library of Congress; 8 Papers of Thomas Jefferson 407).

APPEAL TO ARMS:
THE AMERICAN REVOLUTION

"If we wish to be free...we must fight! An appeal to...the God of hosts, is all that is left us!"

From 1714 until about 1760, Whigs of one shade or another dominated English political affairs. The colonies were for the most part permitted to go their own way, providing their own military protection and paying little in the way of taxes. After 1760, however, Tories came increasingly into power; by 1761, the pro-colonist William Pitt was forced to resign as Prime Minister. A few years thereafter, England acquired vast territories (including Canada) with the end of the Seven Years' War—and found herself with an equally large war debt. British policy toward the colonies rapidly changed. Colonial taxes were to be increased—and fixed in a way that depressed colonial industry—and regular army troops were to be stationed throughout the colonies. In short, the colonies were now to be administered as colonies—for the profit of the mother country. It was a mistake of the first water. Pitt had fought a seven year "war for empire"; his successors would fight a six year one to lose it.

THE ROAD TO REVOLUTION

37. A COLONIAL NEWSPAPER INVOKES THE RIGHT TO BUY ARMS

A British decision to station troops in Boston inspired 'a Journal of the Times,' a colonial propaganda effort prepared in Boston and reprinted widely in colonial newspapers. In the following passage, the anonymous authors defend a vote by Boston colonists requesting their fellow citizens to purchase arms.

> Nor is there a person either in or out of Parliament, who has justly stated and proved one single act of that town, as a public body, to be, we will not say treasonable or seditious, but even at all illegal. … For it is certainly beyond human art and sophistry, to prove the British subjects, to whom the PRIVILEGE of bearing arms is expressly recognized by the Bill of Rights, and who live in a Province where the law requires them to be equipped with ARMS, & c. are guilty of an ILLEGAL ACT, in calling upon one another to be provided with them, as the law directs.

(Boston Evening Post, April 3, 1769)

38. COLONISTS CITE BLACKSTONE ON THE RIGHT TO BEAR ARMS

In the following article, reprinted from a Boston paper, the authors of 'A Journal of the Times' broadly hint that the right to bear arms extends to a right of defense against the royal army.

> Instances of the licentious and outrageous behavior of the military conservators of the peace still multiply upon us, some of which are of such a nature, and have been carried to so great lengths, as must serve fully to evince that a late vote of this town, calling upon the inhabitants to provide themselves with arms for their defense, was a measure as prudent as it was legal; such violences are always to be apprehended from military troops, when quartered in the body of a populous city; but more especially so, when they are lead to believe that they are BECOME NECESSARY TO AWE A SPIRIT OF REBELLION, injuriously said to be existing therein. It is a natural right which the people have reserved to themselves, confirmed by the Bill of Rights, to keep arms for their own defense; and, as Mr. Blackstone observes, it is to be made use of when the sanctions of society and law are found insufficient to restrain the violence of oppression.

(New York Journal Supplement, April 13, 1769)

39. WASHINGTON, MASON, AND OTHERS PLEDGE OWNERSHIP OF ARMS

The Revolutionary spirit found a second home in Virginia. In 1774, the Fairfax County Committee of Safety voted to form a special volunteer militia unit. Its charter, portions of which follow, was drafted by George Mason, later drafter of the Virginia Bill of Rights and member of our Constitutional Convention. Both Mason and George Washington signed the militia charter.

> In this time of extreme danger,...and thoroughly convinced that a well regulated Militia, composed of the Gentlemen, Freeholders and other Freemen, is the natural strength and only safe & stable security of a free government... we the subscribers...have freely and voluntarily agreed...to enroll & embody ourselves into a Militia for this County, intended to consist of all the able-bodied freemen from eighteen to fifty Years of Age.... And such of us have, or can procure Riphel Guns (rifles) & understand the use of them, will be ready to form a Company of marksmen.... Each of us, for ourselves respectively, promise and engage to keep a good fire-lock in proper order, & to furnish Ourselves as soon as possible with, & always keep by us, one pound of Gunpowder, four pounds of Lead, one Dozen gun-flints & a pair of Bullet-moulds....

(K. Rowland, The Life of George Mason, Vol. 1 at 181-82 (1892))

40. THE COLONISTS STOCKPILE HEAVY ARMS

Writing only a few years after the Revolution, William Gordon recalls some of the preparations in Boston.

> The Massachusetts Congress continued their session, and recommended the 16th of March to be observed as the annual day of fasting and prayer.... But they did not presume to rely upon religious exercises in neglect of those civil means which prudence

prescribed. The people, within and without, used every device for conveying safely from Boston into the country all kinds of military articles, which might be wanted in case of a rupture. Cannon balls, and other like heavy stores, were put into carts and carried over the Neck, under the appearence of loads of dung. Half barrels of gun powder were put into butcher's pens, or the hampers of the market people.... Cartridges were packed up in candle boxes and sent off under that deception: but some were at length discovered. The soldiers on the Neck did not make many prizes (captures): however, one day they seized 13,425 musket cartridges with three thousand pound weight of ball....

(W. Gordon, The History of the Rise, Progress and Establishment of the Independence of the United States, Vol. 1 at 473)

41. PATRICK HENRY, REVOLUTIONARY FIREBRAND, CALLS FOR A REVITALIZED MILITIA

Almost every schoolchild knows of Patrick Henry's "Give me liberty or give me death" speech, but few realize the motion to which Henry spoke. The following is a version of the speech reconstructed in later years by Henry's biographer.

The morning of the 23rd of March was opened by reading a petition and memorial from the Assembly of Jamaica 'to the King's most excellent Majesty'.... These proceedings were not adapted to the taste of Mr. Henry.... The House required to be brought up to a bolder tone. He rose therefore, and moved the following manly resolutions:

Resolved, that a well regulated militia, composed of Gentlemen and Yeomen, is the natural strength and only security of a free government....That the establishment of such a militia is, at this time, pecularily necessary....

Resolved, therefore, that this colony be immediately put into a state of defense and that (   ) be a committee to prepare a plan for embodying, arming and disciplining such a number of men as may be sufficient for that purpose.

The alarm which such a proposition must have given to those

who contemplated no resistance of a character more serious than petition, non-importation and passive fortitude, may readily be conceived by the reflecting reader. The shock was painful, it was almost general. (His opponents) urged the late gracious reception of the congressional petition by the Throne....And what was there, they asked, in the situation of the Colony, to tempt us to this? Were we a great military people? Were we ready for war? ....

An ordinary man, in Mr. Henry's situation, would have been glad to compound (compromise) with the displeasure of the House, by being permitted to withdraw his resolutions in silence. Not so Mr. Henry.... The question before the House (Henry said) was one of awful moment for the country. For his own part, he considered it nothing less than a question of freedom or slavery.... If we wish to be free—if we mean to preserve inviolate those inestimable privileges, for which we have been so long contending,... we must fight! I repeat it, sir, we must fight! An appeal to arms, and to the God of hosts, is all that is left us!

(Hezekiah Niles, Republication of the Principles and Acts of the Revolution in America 277-80 (1876))

"THREE MILLION WHIGS, WITH ARMS IN THEIR HANDS"

In 1774, the revolutionary movement entered a new phase when Patriot groups organized a 'purge' of loyalist officers of the militia. The militia elections of that year left scarcely a royalist in command. Control of the militia gave the revolutionary movement an organized base and military machine. Training was expanded, arms and powder stockpiled, and special Minuteman units organized. Lord Percy wrote his superiors to warn that "the opposite party are arming and exercising all over the country".

Britain responded by attempting to disarm the colonists, which generally worsened the situation. In September, 1774, troops stationed in Boston secretly emptied a nearby militia powder magazine. In response approximately 60,000 armed and irate colonists thronged toward Boston, stirred by belief that colonists had been killed and that this was "part of a well designed plan to disarm the people." (S. Patterson, Political Parties in Revolutionary Massachusetts 103 (1973)). In December, 1774, Britain prohibited shipment of guns and ammunition to the colonies: New Hampshire colonists responded by taking over a royal fort and seizing its armory and magazines. The British dilemma was nicely summarized by General Gage: "Though the idea of disarming certain counties was a right one, yet it requires me to be master of the country, in order to enable me to execute it." (The Political Writings of Thomas Paine, vol. 1 at 111 (1856)).

On April 15, Gage made another attempt to disarm the militia, sending a column out from Boston seeking colonist weapons stockpiles. There was a confrontation with the Lexington militia. Someone fired a shot, the troops fired a volley, and the war that would split an empire had begun.

42. A PATRIOT DESCRIBES THE OUTBREAK OF THE REVOLUTION

The fighting which began at Concord soon developed into a miles-long running ambush. The traditional image of clumsily-handled redcoat columns swamped by swarms of snipers is far from accurate, however. The colonists in fact faced a competent foe, who used fast-moving light infantry to protect his flanks and a small cannon to disperse roadblocks. While many colonists did fight as individuals, many more fought as part of militia companies. The British column was badly mauled; at points panic spread and the retreat nearly became a rout. The outcome greatly boosted Patriot morale.

> There were never more than about four hundred provincials together, attacking at one and the same time: and often scarce that number. But as some tired and gave out, others came up. ...The british officers are astonished, chagrined and mortified beyond measure at what has happened. It's death to all their glorying, that their best troops have been obliged to flee before a number of Yankees. ...It can be fully proved that Captain Ford killed five regulars.... A big boy joined in the chase of the retreating troops, and was very expert in firing at them.

(Wm. Gordon, The History of the Rise, Progress and Establishment of the Independence of the United States, Vol. 1 at 484-85)

43. GUERRILLA WAR ON THE FRONTIERS

Most Revolutionary War histories focus upon the dozen or so pitched battles involving the core of the Continental Army. Yet it should be obvious that while this Army was contesting one patch of terrain, something must have dictated who controlled the remainder of America. That something was a guerrilla war, decades before the term came into existence, a war fought by families and small groups. Here the militia excelled. "Seldom has an armed force done so much with so little—providing a vast resevoir of manpower for a multiplicity of military needs, fighting (often unaided by Continentals) in the great majority of the 1,331 land engagements of the war." (Donald Higginbotham, Reconsiderations on the Revolutionary War 103 (1978)). The fight described here is typical of the bulk of those 1,331 unheralded conflicts which determined control of the continent.

Among these brave and active patriots, William Kennedy stood conspicuous.... He was regarded as the best shot with a rifle of any person in all that region. Whether on foot or on horseback, he was never known to miss his aim....

Although he held no Commission, yet the men of the neighborhood acknowledged him as their leader when danger was nigh...and his efforts were often called into requisition by the plundering excursions of the Tories....

On one occasion, a British and Tory scouting party penetrated the settlement, and began their customary work of plundering the women and children of everything they possessed, whether to eat or to wear. One of Kennedy's runners went to the hiding place of Christopher Brandon and two companions—for they were, in the language of the times, out-lyers, and could not with safety stay at home for fear of being massacred by Tories—and notified them....

Reaching the place of meeting, some 15 or 20 had assembled under their leader, Kennedy, and were ready for a hot pursuit. They overtook the Tory band.... The leader of the Tory band, whose name was Neal, was the one singled out and pursued by Kennedy. He fled through an open field, toward the woods, but...quick as thought, the crack of Kennedy's rifle brought Neal tumbling to the ground....More than half the Tory party was killed. 'Not one was taken prisoner,' as Brandon recounted the adventure in his old age, 'for it occurred but seldom—our rifles usually saved us that trouble.'

(Lyman Draper, King's Mountain and its Heroes 129-31 (1881))

44. A BRITISH SOLDIER DISCOVERS THE RISKS OF FORAGING

Universal armament and militia organizations largely precluded British troops from foraging or 'living off the land.' Foraging parties were cut off, supply trains raided, badly needed manpower had to be diverted to protect lines of supply and communication. The result was a logistics problem which, one British historian judges, would have forced Britain out of the war by 1782 even if the main British armies had remained undefeated. (See I. Christie, Crisis of Empire 106 (1966)).

It happened that the garden of a widow woman, which lay between the two camps, was robbed at night. Her son, a mere boy and little for his age, asked leave for finding out and securing the pilferer, in case he should return; which being granted, he concealed himself among the weeds. A British Grenadier, a strapping Highlander, came and filled a large bag; when he had it on his shoulder, the boy left his cover, came softly behind him, cocked his gun and called out to the fellow 'You are my prisoner; if you attempt to throw your bag down I will shoot you dead; go forward on that road'. ... Thus, the boy drove him into the American camp, where he was secured. When the Grenadier ... saw who had made him prisoner, he was most horridly mortified and exclaimed, 'a British Grenadier made prisoner by such a d——d brat!'

(Wm. Gordon, supra, Vol. 2 at 345)

45. PITT TELLS THE HOUSE OF LORDS THE AMERICANS CANNOT BE OVERCOME

William Pitt, the Earl of Chatham, remained the colonist's defender in the House of Lords. Shortly after Concord, he urged attempts at peacemaking.

> (T)he Congress of Philadelphia…do not hold the language of slaves: they tell you what they mean. They do not ask you to repeal your laws as a favor: they claim it as a right; they demand it. They tell you they will not submit to them, and I tell you the (Coercive) Acts must be repealed; you cannot enforce them…. My Lords, there are three millions of whigs. Three millions of whigs, my Lords, with arms in their hands, are a very formitable body. 'twas the whigs, my Lords, that set his Majesty's royal ancestors upon the throne of England. I hope, my Lords, there are yet double the number of whigs in England that there are in America. I hope the whigs of both countries will join and make common cause.

(Wm. Gordon, supra, Vol. 1 at 443)

INDEPENDENCE AND BILLS OF RIGHT

The outbreak of fighting did not instantly dim hopes of retaining a union with Britain; rumors of Whig uprisings there kept colonial hopes of new, Whig, empire alive. By the summer of 1776, however, it was obvious that there would be no Whig takeover. Richard Henry Lee moved that the colonies declare themselves independent, and Thomas Jefferson began to draft a document destined for immortality. Independence, however, left a vacuum—a vacuum filled in many states by promulgation of new state constitutions and bills of rights. Many of these bills recognized a right to self-defense as a fundamental right, and added an express guarantee of a right to keep and bear arms.

46. VIRGINIA DECLARES FOR A WELL-REGULATED MILITIA

Jefferson proposed for Virginia a constitution with elaborate guarantees of freedom, including a provision that no person thereafter entering the state might be held in slavery and that "No freeman shall ever be debarred the use of arms." (Papers of Thomas Jefferson, vol. 1 at 344). The legislature opted for a simpler document written by George Mason.

> A declaration of rights made by the representatives of the good people of Virginia, assembled in full and free convention; which rights do pertain to them and their posterity, as the basis and foundation of government ….

Sec. 13. That a well regulated militia, composed of the body of the people, trained to arms, is the proper, natural and safe defense of a free state; that standing armies, in time of peace, should be avoided, as dangerous to liberty; and that in all cases the military should be under strict subordination to, and governed by, the civil power.

(B. Poore, The Federal and State Constitutions, Colonial Charters and Other Organic Laws (1877))

47. PENNSYLVANIA DECLARES A RIGHT OF CITIZENS TO BEAR ARMS FOR THEMSELVES AND THE STATE

The Pennsylvania Declaration came but a few months after that of Virginia. It set forth a broad right of citizens to bear arms.

A Declaration of the Rights of the Inhabitants of the Commonwealth, on State of Pennsylvania

XIII. That the people have a right to bear arms for the defence of themselves and the state; and as standing armies in the time of peace are dangerous to liberty, they ought not to be kept up; And that the military should be kept under strict subordination to, and governed by, the civil power.

(B. Poore, The Federal and State Constitutions, Colonial Charters and Other Organic Laws (1877))

48. NORTH CAROLINA RECOGNIZES A RIGHT TO BEAR ARMS FOR THE DEFENSE OF THE STATE

North Carolina's 1776 bill of rights likewise protected bearing of arms for the defense of the state; it gave restrictions on standing armies second billing.

A Declaration of Rights

XVII. That the people have a right to bear arms, for the defense of the State; and as standing armies, in time of peace, are dangerous to liberty, they ought not to be kept up; and that the military should be under strict subordination to, and governed by, the civil power.

(B. Poore, The Federal and State Constitutions, Colonial Charters and Other Organic Laws (1877))

49. MASSACHUSETTS RECOGNIZES A RIGHT BOTH TO KEEP

AND TO BEAR ARMS FOR THE COMMON DEFENSE

Massachusetts' 1780 bill of rights was drafted by John Adams, who apparently borrowed from the earlier bills, but added an express recognition of a right to keep arms, albeit for the common defense. Some citizens felt this too narrow. In Northampton, a complaint was made that "the People's right to keep and bear arms...is not expressed with that ample and manly openess and latitude which the importance of the right merits." The critics proposed a "right to keep and bear arms for their own as the common defense." (Smith College Studies in History, vol. 3 at 15(1917)). This sensitivity may explain why the first Congress nine years later refused to add "for the common defense" to the second amendment.

> A Declaration of Rights of the Inhabitants of the
> Commonwealth of Massachusetts
> Art. XVII. The people have a right to keep and to bear arms for the common defense. And as, in time of peace, armies are dangerous to liberty, they ought not to be maintained without the consent of the legislature; and the military power shall always be held in an exact subordination to the civil authority and be governed by it.

(B. Poore, The Federal and State Constitutions, Colonial Charters and Other Organic Laws (1877))

The state declarations of rights of the Revolutionary period thus reflected an American consensus that arms-bearing was a vital right of free men. Later declarations recognized this right in still more unequivocal terms. Pennsylvania's 1790 constitution gave further emphasis to the right, already protected by the 1776 declaration: "That the general, great and essential prinicples of liberty and free government may be recognized and unalterably established, we declare.... Sec. 21. That the right of citizens to bear arms, in defense of themselves and the State, shall not be questioned." Kentucky's 1792 constitution, drafted with the detailed advice of James Madison, similarly provided "That the right of the citizens to bear arms in defense of themselves and the State shall not be questioned."

The decision of 1776 raised questions beyond the State constitutions, however. The foremost question concerned the structure of a national government. This is turn renewed, on a still grander scale, the issue of citizens' rights.

A NATIONAL CONSTITUTION—
BUT NO BILL OF RIGHTS

"To preserve liberty, it is essential that the whole body of the people always possess arms, and be taught alike, especially when young, how to use them."

Even prior to the Declaration of Independence, the Continental Congress had begun work on the Articles of Confederation, which laid the groundwork for an American nation. The Articles, however, gave only very limited power to the national government. There was no national executive or judicial branch, little direct power to enforce treaties, and Congress required a two-thirds majority for any action.

In February 1787 the Congress resolved in favor of calling a convention 'for the sole and express purpose of revising the Articles of Confederation...' The delegates to the convention exceeded this authority and drafted an entirely new system, to be effective when ratified by nine states.

Not all were pleased with the new proposal. Both Virginia delegates to the Constitutional Convention—Richard Henry Lee and George Mason—refused to sign the final draft and left in disgust to organize an opposition. The refusal of the Convention to add a Bill of Rights was central to their dissatisfaction, in which they were joined by such powerful figures as Patrick Henry and to a lesser extent Thomas Jefferson.

The proposed constitution provided that it would take effect only if nine states ratified. Most states called special conventions (recorded, with greater or with less skill by local recorders) to cast their vote.

The conflict over ratification lay between groups which came to be known as Federalists, who favored ratification, and Antifederalists, who did not. The arguments of both sides relied heavily upon universal citizen armament. Antifederalists argued that the lack of a constitutional protection for such armament was a critical flaw; Federalists asserted that (whatever the flaws of the constitution) the fact that all citizens were armed ruled out a new tyranny and made ratification safe. The conflict produced concrete results as ratifying conventions began to add calls for a Bill of Rights to their ratifications

THE FEDERALIST VIEW

50. NOAH WEBSTER: ARMS OWNERSHIP AS A SECURITY FOR RATIFICATION

Webster's 'Examination' was one of the first pamphlets written in support of the proposed constitution. The original bears his endorsement that "this is a hasty production, written at the request of Mr. Fitzsimmons of Philidelphia, a member of the Convention." In it, Webster supports ratification against claims that the constitution improperly failed to limit standing armies. Such could never be a problem, Webster argues, where all citizens were armed.

> Another source of power in government is a military force. But this, to be efficient, must be superior to any force that exists among the people, or which they can command; otherwise, this force would be annihilated on first exercise of acts of oppression. Before a standing army can rule, the people must be disarmed, as they are in almost every kingdom in Europe. The supreme power in America cannot enforce unjust laws by the sword, because the whole body of the people are armed, and constitute a force superior to any band of regular troops that can be, on any pretence, raised in the United States.

(Noah Webster, 'An Examination into the Leading Principles of the Federal Constitution Proposed by the Late Convention Held at Philidelphia,' reprinted in Pamphlets on the Constitution of the United States 56 (1888))

51. MADISON, IN FEDERALIST NO. 46, ECHOES WEBSTER

Critics of the proposed constitution continued to raise its failure to limit the federal power to raise and support a standing army. In Federalist No. 46, Madison met the argument directly, arguing that the failure to limit standing armies was no flaw at all: the American 'advantage of being armed' ensured against any misuse, and made such protection superfluous.

> The only refuge left for those who prophesy the downfall of the State governments is the visionary supposition that the federal government may previously accumulate a military force for the projects of ambition.... The highest number to which, according to the best computation, a standing army can be carried in any country does not exceed one-hundredth part of the whole number of souls; or one twenty-fifth part of the number able to bear arms. This proportion would not yield, in the United States, an army of more than twenty-five or thirty thousand men. To these would be opposed a militia amounting to near half a million of citizens with arms in their hands.... It may well be doubted whether a militia thus circumstanced could ever be conquered by such a proportion of regular troops. Those who are best acquainted with the late successful resistance of this country against the British arms will be most inclined to deny the possibility of it. Besides the advantage of being armed, which the Americans possess over the people of almost every other nation, the existance of subordinate governments (in the states) forms a barrier against the enterprises of ambition, more insurmountable than any which a simple government of any form can admit of. Notwithstanding the military establishments in the several kingdoms of Europe, which are carried as far as the public resources will bear, the governments are afraid to trust the people with arms.

(James Madison, The Federalist, No. 46)

THE ANTIFEDERALIST VIEW

52. RICHARD HENRY LEE: "IT IS ESSENTIAL THAT THE WHOLE BODY OF THE PEOPLE ALWAYS POSSESS ARMS"

Richard Henry Lee long remained at the spearhead of American liberties. In the Continental Congress, he was the first to move that the colonies declare independence. He was the first national figure to stress the proposed constitution's lack of a Bill of Rights. He then, as Senator in the first Congress, had the privilege of voting on the Bill of Rights he did so much to create. His pamphlet, Letters from the Federal Farmer, was the most widely-read antifederalist publication of the time; federalists complained of its impact not only in Virginia, but in Massachusetts, Pennsylvania and Connecticut. (J. Goebel, History of the Supreme Court of the United States vol.1 at 287-88). In the portion which follows, Lee not only stresses the role of armed citizens, but rejects 'select militias' made up of only a part of the people. To Lee and his contemporaries, 'militia' meant an armed people, not selected units such as the earlier Minutemen and the modern National Guard.

> To preserve liberty, it is essential that the whole body of the people always possess arms, and be taught alike, especially when young, how to use them....
>
> It is true, the yeomenry of the country possess the lands, the weight of property, possess arms, and are too strong a body of men to be openly offended (but) they may in twenty or thirty years be, by means imperceptable to them, totally deprived of that boasted weight and strength. This may be done in great measure by Congress, if disposed to do it, by modeling the militia. Should one-fifth or one-eighth part of the men capable of bearing arms be made into a select militia, as has been proposed...and all the others put upon a plan which will render them of no importance, the former will answer all the purposes of an army, while the latter will be defenseless....
>
> (T)he constitution ought to secure a genuine, and guard against a select, militia, by providing that the militia shall always be kept well organized, armed and disciplined, and include, according

to the past and general usage of the States, all men capable of bearing arms; and that all regulations tending to render this militia useless and defenselesss, by establishing select corps of militia, or distinct bodies of military men not having any permanent interest and attachments in the community, to be avoided....

(Richard Henry Lee, Letters from the Federal Farmer to the Republican)

53. GEORGE MASON AND PATRICK HENRY: "THE GREAT OBJECT IS THAT EVERY MAN BE ARMED"

The Virginia ratifying convention boasted an impressive intellectual representation. Heading the antifederalists were George Mason, author of the Virginia constitution and Bill of Rights, and Patrick Henry, patriot orator and wartime governor of the state. Both stressed the role of the militia—Henry arguing in the alternate that the national government might either fail to provide for arming the militia, or might deliberately make the armament duties so burdensome that people would turn to a standing army instead.

> (Mason) An instance within the memory of some of this House, will show us how our militia may be destroyed. Forty years ago, when the resolution of enslaving America was formed in Great Britain, the British Parliament was advised by an artful man, who was governor of Pennsylvania, to disarm the people—that was the most effectual way to enslave them—but they should not do it openly; but to weaken them and let them sink gradually, by totally disusing and neglecting the militia.
>
> (Henry) The militia, sir, is our ultimate safety. We can have no security without it.... The great object is that every man be armed...everyone who is able may have a gun. But have we not learned by experience, that necessary as it is to have arms, and though our Assembly has, by a succession of laws for many years, endeavored to have the militia completely armed, it is still very far from being the case?

(David Robertson, Debates and Other Proceedings of the Convention of Virginia, at 270, 274-74 (2d ed. 1805))

THE STATE CONVENTIONS
DEMAND A BILL OF RIGHTS

The federalist hope had been to obtain a ratification vote before opposition had time to muster. In Delaware, for instance, the convention unanimously ratified after only four days of consideration. From that point onward, opposition to the proposed constitution grew—and with it grew proposals for a Bill of Rights. These proposals thus reflect what the American people demanded as a price of ratification. Moreover, these represent the actual raw material from which the Bill of Rights was later composed, since Madison in drafting it worked from a pamphlet reprinting these demands.

54. PENNSYLVANIA DELEGATES CALL FOR A BILL OF RIGHTS GUARANTEEING ARMS FOR DEFENSE AND HUNTING

The Pennsylvania convention saw the first drive to demand a bill of rights as a price of ratification. While this failed, it mustered a substantial number of votes. Copies of the Pennsylvania proposals were quickly sent to members of the remaining conventions, and thus served as a catalyst for later demands. The Pennsylvania proposal, which speaks of a right to 'bear arms' for self-defense and hunting, incidentally demonstrates that 'bear arms' was not a term of art relating only to military service.

> 6. That the people have a right to freedom of speech, of writing, and of publishing their sentiments, therefore, the freedom of the press shall not be restrained by any law of the United States.
>
> 7. That the people have a right to bear arms for the defense of themselves and their own state, or the United States, or for the purpose of killing game; and no law shall be passed for disarming the people or any of them, unless for crimes committed, or real danger of public harm from individuals; and as standing armies in the time of peace are dangerous to liberty, they ought not to be kept up; and that the military shall be kept under strict subordination to and be governed by the civil power.

(J. McMaster & F. Stone, eds., Pennsylvania and the Federal Constitution 187-88, at 422 (1888))

55. SAM ADAMS CALLS FOR A BILL OF RIGHTS TO PROTECT CITIZENS' "OWN ARMS"

Samuel Adams had done as much as any man to bring on the Revolution. As a delegate to his state's ratifying convention, he initially opposed ratification, then drafted a proposal for a bill of rights as a compromise. Federalists in the convention strongly opposed the motion, and Adams was unsuccessful.

> ...and that the said Constitution be never construed to infringe the just liberty of the press or the rights of conscience; or to prevent the people of the United States who are peaceable citizens from keeping their own arms; or to raise standing armies, unless when necessary for the defense of the United States or of some one or more of them; or to prevent the people from petitioning, in a peaceable and orderly manner, the Federal Legislature for a redress of grievances; or to subject the people to unreasonable searches and seizures of their persons, papers or possessions.

(Pierce & Hale, eds., Debates and Proceedings in the Convention of the Commonwealth of Massachusetts, at 86-87 (Boston, 1850))

56. NEW HAMPSHIRE CALLS FOR A GUARANTEE THAT "CONGRESS SHALL NEVER DISARM ANY CITIZEN"

The Constitution had provided that it would bind the ratifying states only if nine or more ratified. New Hampshire's convention gave it the critical ninth vote—but with a demand for a bill of rights.

> XI. Congress shall make no laws touching religion, or to infringe the rights of conscience.
> XII. Congress shall never disarm any citizen, unless such as are or have been in actual rebellion.

(J. Elliot, Debates in the Several State Conventions on the Adoption of the Federal Constitution, Vol. 1 at 326 (2d ed. 1836))

57. VIRGINIA AND NEW YORK CALL FOR RECOGNITION OF "A RIGHT TO KEEP AND BEAR ARMS"

Even with nine states, the Constitution would not long survive without the agreement of Virginia and New York, the intellectual and commercial centers of the former colonies. Here, too, ratification was prefaced with a call for a Bill of Rights. The proposals—which are clear reflections of the wording of the later Second Amendment—show an origin in the state bills of rights of 1776-1780. From the Virginia bill came the "well regulated militia"; from Massachusetts came the right both to keep and to bear arms—but without the restriction "for the common defense".

> (Virginia) Seventeenth, that the people have a right to keep and bear arms; that a well regulated militia composed of the body of the people trained to arms is the proper, natural, and safe defense of a free state.
> (New York)That the people have the right to keep and bear arms; that a well regulated militia, including the body of the people capable of bearing arms, is the proper, natural and safe defense of a free state.

(Documents Illustrative of the Formation of the Union of the American States 1030, 1035 (1927))

Thus the United States had a Constitution—accompanied by a demand that it be promptly amended with a Bill of Rights. The call of so many influential states could not be easily disregarded—nor could Patrick Henry's call for a second constitutional convention to remedy the errors of the first.

THE DRAFTING OF THE BILL OF RIGHTS

"A well-regulated militia...being the best security of a free State, the right of the people to keep and bear arms shall not be infringed..."

James Madison knew firsthand the force behind the demand for a Bill of Rights. He had publicly opposed insertion of a Bill of Rights in the original constitution, and as a result was passed over for a seat in the first Senate. When he ran for the House, his district was 'gerrymandered' to his great disadvantage. Madison won the uphill electoral fight only after making numerous promises to press for a bill of rights in the first Congress. One of history's paradoxes is that the drafter of the American Bill of Rights was one of its original opponents.

In drafting the Bill of Rights, Madison did not write upon a clean slate. The state conventions had very nicely set out the protections which the people demanded. Madison simply purchased a pamphlet which listed the demands of the state conventions. (Rutland & Hobson, eds. 12 Papers of James Madison 58). Of over two hundred rights therein listed, Madison chose a total of nineteen for express listing, adding clauses stating that recognition of these nineteen rights was not meant to rule out others.

58. IN THE FIRST CONGRESS, JAMES MADISON INTRODUCES A BILL OF RIGHTS

Madison's initial Bill of Rights proposals have two features which merit comment. First, contrary to some claims that 'right of the people' connoted a state rather than individual right, Madison's plan used 'right of the people' to describe freedom of speech, press and other clearly individual rights.

A second noteworthy aspect of Madison's plan is its organization. Today, of course, we are accustomed to a Bill of Rights structured as a number of amendments, generally printed following the Constitution. But Madison envisioned amendments written to be interlineated with the Constitution's text. Thus we can determine exactly the context in which each right was seen. If Madison had seen the right to bear arms as primarily restricting federal power over state militia, he probably would have designated it as an amendment to Article I, sec. 8, which contains the federal power to organize and call out the militia. Instead, he grouped the right to keep and bear arms with freedom of speech and similar rights and placed it after Article I, sec. 9. There, it would follow the guarantees of individual rights in the original Constitution (viz., limitations on suspension of habeus corpus and enactment of bills of attainder or ex post facto laws).

> The amendments which have occurred to me, proper to be recommended by Congress to the state legislatures, are these:
>
> First, that there be prefixed to the Constitution a declaration, that all power is originally vested in, and consequently derived from, the people....

(Two amendments relating to the number and pay of Representatives follow)

> Fourthly, that in article 1st, section 9, between clauses 3 and 4, there be inserted these clauses, to wit: ...The people shall not be deprived or abridged of their right to speak, to write, or to publish their sentiments; and the freedom of the press, as one of the great bulwarks of liberty, shall be invincible.
>
> The people shall not be restrained from peaceably assembling and consulting for the common good....
>
> The right of the people to keep and bear arms shall not be infringed; a well armed and well regulated militia being the best security of a free country; but no person religiously scrupulous of bearing arms shall be compelled to render military service in person....

(1 Debates and Proceedings in the Congress of the United States 433-34)

59. MADISON'S NOTES: 1688 DECLARATION INSUFFICIENT

Possibly because he was pressed for time, or because of poor reporting, the official report of Madison's speech to the House gives no insight into the extent of the freedoms which he listed. However, among his papers is an interesting note headed, in his hand, "J.M.'s notes for speaking for amendts in Congress 1789." Madison preferred to speak from notes, which he habitually stored in his hat; the note is scribbled on a scrap about five inches by three. This may well be the very paper that Madison held as he explained the Bill of Rights to the House.

One portion relates to an argument that the English 1688 Declaration of Rights, and thus the common law, was an inadequate guarantee of individual rights. Madison's note strongly suggests that he meant the Bill of Rights to protect the same individual right to own arms mentioned in the Declaration—but without the Declaration's limitation of the right to protestants.

> Read the amendments—
> They relate 1st to private rights—
> Bill of rights—useful—not essential—
> Fallacy on both sides—especy. as to English Decln. of Rts—
> 1. Mere act of Parlt.
> 2. No freedom of press-conscience-genl. warrants—habs.
> corpus—jury in civil cases—criml. attainders—Arms to
> protestts.

(Madison papers, Library of Congress manuscript collection—reproduced in 12 Papers of James Madison 193)

60. THE COMMITTEE OF ELEVEN REPORTS A BILL OF RIGHTS

Madison's proposals were referred to a Committee of Eleven, which retained his plan of interweaving the amendments with the text of the Constitution. The committee generally cut back on Madison's language, and reversed the order of clauses in his right to keep and bear arms proposal.

Mr. Vining, from the Committee of eleven, to whom it was

referred to take the subject of amendments...and to report thereupon, made a report, which was read, and is as followeth:

Art. I, Sec. 9—Between Par. 2 and 3, insert: 'No religion shall
be established by law, nor shall the equal rights of conscience be
infringed.

The freedom of speech, and of the press, and the right of the
people peaceably to assemble and consult for their common
good, and to apply to the government for redress of grievances,
shall not be infringed.

A well-regulated militia, composed of the body of the people,
being the best security of a free State, the right of the people to
keep and bear arms shall not be infringed, but no person rel-
giously scrupulous shall be compelled to bear arms....

(Documentary History of the Constitution of the United States, Vol. 5 at
186-87 (1905))

61. THE HOUSE DEBATES THE BILL OF RIGHTS

The House accepted the right to keep and bear arms proposal with
little controversy. Such acquiescence was not typical of the entire Bill:
the clauses forbidding establishment of a religion inspired some debate
over whether they might injure religion; the protection of the right to assemble and petition met some particularly strong opposition from legislators who feared it would require them to vote in accord with petitions
so submitted. What dispute there was on the bearing of arms focused upon
the clause protecting conscientious objection, not over the right to keep
arms itself. The value of the floor debates is further attenuated by the the
fact that they were largely monopolized by Gerry, a rambling speaker with
little apparent understanding.

Mr. Gerry. This Declaration of Rights, I take it, is intended to
secure the people against the maladministration of government;
if we could suppose that, in all cases, the rights of the people
would be attended to, the occasion for guards of this type would
be removed. Now, I am apprehensive, sir, that this clause would
give an opportunity to the people in power to destroy the Constitution itself. They can declare who are those religiously scru-

pulous, and prevent them from bearing arms.

What, sir, is the use of a militia? It is to prevent the establishment of a standing army, the bane of liberty. Now, it must be evident that, under this provision, together with their other powers, Congress could take such measures with respect to a militia, as to make a standing army necessary. Whenever governments mean to invade the rights and liberties of the people, they always attempt to destroy the militia....

Mr. Seney wished to know what question there was before the committee, in order to ascertain the point upon which the gentleman was speaking.

Mr. Gerry replied that he meant to make a motion, as he disapproved of the words as they stood. He then proceeded. ...Now, if we give a discretionary power to exclude those from militia duty who have religious scruples, we may as well make no provision on this head....

Mr. Jackson did not expect that the people of the United States would all turn Quakers or Moravians; one part would have to defend the others in event of an invasion. Now this, in his opinion, was unjust, unless the Constitution secured an equivalent (required payment for a substitute)....

Mr. Smith, of South Carolina, inquired what were the words used by the conventions respecting this amendment. If the gentleman would conform to what was proposed by Virginia and Carolina, he would second him. He thought they were to be excused provided they found a substitute....

Mr. Benson moved to have the words 'but no person religiously scrupulous shall be compelled to bear arms' struck out. He would always leave it to the benevolence of the legislature....

The motion for striking the whole clause being seconded was put, and decided in the negative—22 members voting for it, and 24 against it.

Mr. Gerry objected to the first part of the clause, on account of the uncertainty with which it was expressed. A well regulated militia being the best security of a free state, admitted an idea that a standing army was a secondary one....

Mr. Gerry's motion not being seconded, the question was put on the clause as reported, which being adopted;

Mr. Burke proposed to add to the clause just agreed to, an

amendment to the following effect: 'A standing army of regular troops in time of peace is dangerous to public liberty, and such shall not be raised or kept up in time of peace but from necessity and for the security of the people, nor then without the consent of two-thirds of the members present in both Houses; and in all cases the military shall be subordinate to the civil authority.' This being seconded,...

Mr. Hartley thought the amendment in order and was ready to give his opinion on it. He hoped the people of America would always be satisfied with having a majority to govern. He never wished to see two-thirds or three-quarters required, because it might put it in the power of a small minority to govern the whole Union.

The question on Mr. Burke's motion was put, and lost by a majority of thirteen.'

(1 Debates and Proceedings, supra, at 749-51)

62. THE SENATE AMENDS THE BILL OF RIGHTS

No record was kept of Senate debates until 1794. As a result, we do not know the substance of that body's deliberations on the Bill of Rights. The situation is further complicated by the notorious inaccuracy of the Senate Journal in which, for instance, the final wording of the right to keep and bear arms does not tally with the reported amendments. The Journal does clearly show that the Senate did reject an attempted amendment which would have recognized only a right to keep and bear arms 'for the common defense'. The conflict over insertion of a similar clause in the Massachusetts bill of rights (supra, para. 54) suggests that the possible effects of such an amendment were well understood. It is also interesting that a provision stating that standing armies ought to be avoided was defeated, suggesting that while fear of such armies may have been part of the rationale for recognizing a right to bear arms, it was not the core concern.

Tuesday, August 25, 1789....
The resolve of the House of Representatives of the 24th of August, was read, as followeth:...
Articles in addition to, and amendment of, the constitution of the United States....

Art. V. A well regulated militia, composed of the body of the people, being the best security of a free state, the right of the people to keep and bear arms, shall not be infringed, but no one religiously scrupulous of bearing arms shall be compelled to render military service in person.

Friday, September 4, 1789....

On motion, upon the fifth article, to subjoin the following proposition, to wit: 'That standing armies, in time of peace, being dangerous to liberty, should be avoided....' ...it passed in the negative.

On motion to adopt the fifth article of the amendments proposed by the House of Representatives, amended to read as followeth: 'a well regulated militia, being the best security of a free state, the right of the people to keep and bear arms, shall not be infringed:' it passed in the affirmative.

Wednesday, September 9, 1789.

On motion to strike out the fourth article: it passed in the affirmative.

On motion to amend article the fifth, by inserting the words 'for the common defense,' next to the words 'bear arms:' it passed in the negative.

On motion, on article the fifth, to strike the word 'fifth' after 'article the,' and insert 'fourth,' and to amend the article to read as follows: 'A well regulated militia being the security of a free state, the right of the people to keep and bear arms shall not be infringed,' it passed in the affirmative.

(Journal of the First Session of the Senate, 63-64, 77 (1820))

The right to keep and bear arms, without any restriction to the 'common defense', thus became the fourth of twelve amendments presented to state legislatures for ratification. When the first two proposed amendments failed to secure enough ratifications, the right to keep and bear arms became the Second Amendment to the Constitution.

CONTEMPORARY DISCUSSIONS OF THE SECOND AMENDMENT

"Wherever standing armies are kept up, and the right of the people to keep and bear arms is, under any color or pretext whatsoever, prohibited, liberty, if not already annihilated, is on the brink of destruction."

Records of what 18th century Americans thought of the Bill of Rights are surprisingly rare. Members of the first Congress, who might have been expected to write at length, contented themselves in every extant letter with brief statements of their overall position, pro or con, on passage. Possibly the event was overshadowed by the recent conflict over ratification, by the present need to form the government of a new nation, or by fears of Patrick Henry's unsuccessful drive for a second constitutional convention. Nonetheless, some contemporaries of the framers, who had special insights into their purposes, did produce discussions of the Bill of Rights in relation to the right to keep and bear arms.

63. A FRIEND OF MADISON DEFENDS THE SECOND AMENDMENT AS A PROTECTION FOR 'PRIVATE ARMS'

Tench Coxe, who signed himself 'A Pennsylvanian,' was a prominent federalist writer and personal friend of Madison. Shortly after Madison introduced his bill, Coxe published the following article in the Federal Gazette, the most prominent federalist newspaper. He sent a copy to Madison, with a note that "It has appeared to me that a few well-tempered observations on these proposals might have a good effect. I have therefore...thrown together a few remarks on the first part of the resolutions...It is in the Fed. Gazette of 18th instant." (12 James Madison Papers 239). On June 24, 1789, Madison sent his thanks, adding that "the printed remarks I already find in the gazettes here" and expressing his belief that the drive for a bill of rights would "be greatly favored by explanatory strictures of a healing tendency, and is therefore already indebted to the cooperation of your pen." (12 James Madison Papers 257). Coxe's article is thus uniquely authoritative. It is a contemporary explanation, published in the most prominent political daily of the time, reprinted by journals in the city where the first Congress sat, and given an immediate imprimatur by Madison himself.

REMARKS ON THE FIRST PART OF THE AMENDMENTS TO THE FEDERAL CONSTITUTION, MOVED ON THE 8TH INSTANT IN THE HOUSE OF REPRESENTATIVES.

The next article establishes religious liberty, and all those political rights, which by various tricks of states have been wounded through its means, on the firmest ground. The tender, almost sacred rights of conscience, says this inestimable article, shall by no means, on no account be abridged or interfered with. No self righteous or powerful church shall ever set up its impious dominion over all the rest. Every pious man may pay to the divine author of his existence the tribute of thanksgiving and adoration, in the manner of his forefathers.

The following paragraph declares the freedom of the press to be a main bulwark of liberty, and reasoning unanswerably from its usefulness and indispensible necessity, declares that it shall be inviolable.

As civil rulers, not having their duty to the people before them, may attempt to tyrannize, and as the military forces which must occasionally be raised to defend our country, might pervert their power to the injury of their fellow-citizens, the people are confirmed by the next article in their right to keep and bear their private arms.

(The Federal Gazette and Philidelphia Evening Post , June 18, 1789, p.2)

64. ST. GEORGE TUCKER, FRIEND OF JEFFERSON AND MADISON, SUMMARIZES THE SECOND AMENDMENT

It is probably fair to say that St. George Tucker knew more of the intended legal effect of the Bill of Rights than any American before or since. A twice-wounded Revolutionary War veteran, law professor at William and Mary, he was appointed to Virginia's highest court by Thomas Jefferson and to its federal district court by James Madison. A modern commentator has observed that Tucker "was in a particularly good position to follow the formation of the federal government because of his attendance at the Annapolis Convention and his friendship with many who participated in the framing of the federal Constitution. ...His brother Thomas Tudor Tucker went to the House of Representatives from South Carolina in 1789, and Tucker's good friend John Page was elected from Virginia the same year. Through a frequent correspondence with both, the judge was able to stay informed of the important political debates of the day." (W. Bryson, Legal Education in Virginia 670 (1982)). In 1803, Tucker published an edition of Blackstone annotated to American law. His work enjoyed a unique prestige among his contemporaries: for a quarter of a century he remained the legal commenator most frequently cited by the Supreme Court (W. Bryson, Legal Education in Virginia 682 (1982)); Jefferson described his book as "the last perfect digest of both branches of law" (W. Bryson, Legal Education in Virginia 26 (1982)); after his death, a British periodical mentioned his long reputation as "the American Blackstone." (E. Bauer, Commentaries on the Constitution 1790 – 1960, at 181 (1965)). Tucker's reference to the second amendment as "Art. 4" emphasizes the contemporaneous quality of his work. The bill of rights proposed by Congress included 12 amendments, the first two of which ultimately went unratified. But these first two were still open for ratification, so many nineteenth century jurists—including John

Marshall—numbered what we today call the second amendment as amendment four, the fourth as amendment six, and so on. (W. Swindler, Sources and Documents of U.S. Constitutions, Vol. 1 at 415 (1982))

5. The fifth and last auxiliary right of the subject, that I shall at present mention, is that of having arms for their defense /40/ suitable to their condition and degree, and as allowed by law /41/....

(Tucker's annotation)

40) The right of the people to keep and bear arms shall not be infringed. Amendments to C., U.S., Art. 4 (sic—apparently using the original numbering), and this without qualification as to their condition or degree, as is the case in the British government.

41) Whoever examines the forest and game laws in the British code, will readily perceive that the right of keeping arms is effectually taken away from the people of England. The commentator himself informs us, Vol.II, p.412, that 'the prevention of popular insurrections and resistance to government by disarming the bulk of the people, is a reason oftener meant than avowed by the makers of the forest and game laws.'

(Tucker's Appendix on American law)

8. A well regulated militia being necessary to the security of a free state, the right of the people to keep and bear arms, shall not be infringed. Amendments to C. U.S., Art. 4.

This may be regarded as the true palladium of liberty. The right of self defense is the first law of nature; in most governments it has been the study of rulers to confine this right within the narrowest limits possible. Wherever standing armies are kept up, and the right of the people to keep and bear arms is, under any color or pretext whatsoever, prohibited, liberty, if not already annihilated, is on the brink of destruction. In England, the people have been disarmed, generally under the specious pretext of preserving the game.... True it is, their bill of rights seems at first view to counteract this policy, but the right of bearing arms is limited to protestants, and the words suitable to their condition and degree, have been interpreted...so that not one man in five hundred can keep a gun in his house without being subject to a penalty..

(St. George Tucker, ed., Blackstone's Commentaries, With Notes of Reference to the Constitution and Laws, at 143, 300 (1803))

Tucker's reference to the Hunting Acts as disarming the British during his time period reflects a misunderstanding common at the time. As noted above, the 1692 and 1707 amendments allowed seizure only of guns actually used to break the law, although non-gun hunting implements and dogs could be seized, without proof of any lawbreaking, from anyone not legally qualified to hunt. But the complexity of the law made for many such misunderstandings; when a judge of King's Bench was asked in 1782 to construe the Hunting Act, he proclaimed candidly that "the Act, as it stands, is nonsense." (P.B. Munsche, Gentlemen and Poachers: The English Games Laws 1671-1831, at 9 (1981)).

65. WILLIAM RAWLE, FRIEND OF WASHINGTON: SECOND AMENDMENT ELIMINATES ANY "POWER TO DISARM THE PEOPLE."

William Rawle's background sharply contrasts with that of Tucker. A suspected Tory, Rawle studied law in England during the Revolution. Yet after the war Washington came to appreciate his legal talent and offered to appoint him first Attorney General of the United States. Rawle declined for personal reasons, and instead became United States Attorney for Pennsylvania. (David Brown, Eulogium Upon Wìlliam Rawle, 8-9,15 (Philadelphia, 1837)). Like Tucker, Rawle had close personal knowledge of the framers' views. His acquaintance with Washington, Franklin and others probably came from his membership in Franklin's 'Society for Political Inquiries' which met during the Constitutional Convention; as Secretary to the Library Company of Philadelphia, he had personally invited each Convention member to use the facilities; he later sat in the Pennsylvania legislature which ratified the federal bill of rights. (E. Bauer, Commentators on the Constitution 1790-1960, at 61 (1965)). In 1825, he published his 'View of the Constitution,' which quickly went through three editions and became the constitutional law textbook for many early American law schools; it was the standard constitutional text at Harvard until 1845, and at Dartmouth until 1860. (E. Bauer, Commentators on the Constitution 1790-1960, at 350; 4 Memoirs of the Hist. Soc. of Pa. 63 (1840)). Rawle treats the second amendment's militia clause as entirely separable from its right to keep and bear arms clause; to him, the latter is unquestionably an individual right, and one broader than allowed at common law.

> In the Second Article, it is declared, that a well regulated militia is necessary to the security of a free state; a proposition from which few will dissent. Although in actual war, the services of regular troops are confessedly more valuable, yet while peace prevails, and in the commencement of a war before a regular force can be raised, the militia form the palladium of the country....
>
> The corollary from the first position is, that the right of the people to keep and bear arms shall not be infringed. The prohibition is general. No clause in the Constitution could by any rule of construction be conceived to give the Congress a power to disarm the people. Such a flagitious attempt could only be made under some general pretence by a state legislature. But if in any blind pursuit of inordinate power either should attempt it, this amendment may be appealed to as a restraint on both.
>
> In most of the countries of Europe, this right does not seem to be denied, although it is allowed more or less sparingly, according to the circumstances. In England, a country which boasts so much of its freedom, the right was assured to protestant subjects only, and it is cautiously described to be that of bearing arms for their defense 'suitable to their conditions, and as allowed by law'. An arbitrary code for the preservation of game in that country has long disgraced them.

(Wm. Rawle, A View of the Constitution 125 (2d ed. 1829))

66. JUSTICE STORY ON THE BEARING OF ARMS

Joseph Story was appointed to the United States Supreme Court by James Madison. During his 34 years of service, he also served as professor of law at Harvard and prepared his famed Commentaries.

> The importance of this article will scarcely be doubted by any persons who have duly reflected upon the subject. The militia is the natural defense of a free country....The right of the citizens to keep and bear arms has justly been considered as the palladium of the liberties of a Republic; since it offers a strong moral check

against the usurpation and arbitrary power of rulers and will generally, even if these are successful in the first instance, enable to people to resist and triumph over them....

A similar provision in favor of protestants (for to them it is confined) is to be found in the bill of rights of 1688, it being declared 'the subjects, which are protestants, may have arms for their defense suitable to their condition, and as allowed by law.' But under various pretences the effect of this provision has been greatly narrowed; and it is at present in England more nominal than real as a defensive privilege.

(Joseph Story, Commentaries on the Constitution of the United States, Vol. 3 at 746-47 (1833))

67. THOMAS COOLEY EXPRESSLY REJECTS THE COLLECTIVE RIGHTS VIEW

Thomas Cooley was not a contemporary of the framers, except in the most liberal sense of the term—Jefferson died when Cooley was two years of age. He was, however, probably the most widely respected legal commentator of the following generations. He writes from the standpoint of an age that was increasingly concerned with controlling rather than protecting the exercise of rights—yet clearly rejects a narrowing interpretation of the second amendment.

The right of assembly always was, and still is, subject to reasonable regulations by law. Parliament has sometimes been compelled to interpose strict regulations, when a great and tumultuous body of people threatened to appear at its door to present a demand for a change in the law.

The right to petition is not coextensive with the right to assemble.... A petition is, nevertheless, merely a privileged publication, and the right to be heard by means of it may be so abused as to take away the privilege....

The second amendment... like most other provisions in the Constitution, has a history. It was adopted, with some modification and enlargement, from the English Bill of Rights of 1688, where it stood as a protest against the arbitrary action of the overturned dynasty in disarming the people, and as a pledge of the new rulers that this tyrannical action should cease....

The right is general. It may be supposed from the phraseology of this provision that the right to keep and bear arms was only guaranteed to the militia; but this would be an interpretation not warranted by the intent. The militia, as has been explained elsewhere, consists of those persons who, under the law, are liable to the performance of military duty, and are officered and enrolled for service when called upon....(I)f the right were limited to those enrolled, the purpose of the guarantee might be defeated altogether by the action or the neglect to act of the government it was meant to hold in check. The meaning of the provision undoubtedly is, that the people, from whom the militia must be taken, shall have the right to keep and bear arms, and they need no permission or regulation of law for the purpose. But this enables the government to have a well regulated militia; for to bear arms implies something more than mere keeping; it implies the learning to handle and use them in a way that makes those who keep them ready for their efficient use; in other words, it implies the right to meet for voluntary discipline in arms, observing in so doing the laws of public order.

(Thomas Cooley, General Principles of Constitutional Law 298-99 (3d. ed. 1898))

THE RIGHT TO KEEP AND BEAR ARMS IN THE COURTS

"The right of whole people...to keep and bear arms...and not such merely as are used by the militia, shall not be infringed..."

Early judicial interpretations of the right to keep and bear arms come almost exclusively from the state courts. The reason is simple: there were no federal arms laws to challenge.

WHAT IS THE NATURE OF THE RIGHT?

68. THE RIGHT AS AN ABSOLUTE: KENTUCKY VOIDS A CONCEALED WEAPONS STATUTE

In 1813, Kentucky and Louisiana adopted the first American bans on carrying of concealed weapons. In 1822, the Court of Appeals, the state's highest court, voided the statute.

> The indictment, in the words of the Act, charges Bliss with having worn concealed as a weapon, a sword in a cane....
> In argument, the judgement was assailed by the counsel of Bliss, exclusively on the ground of the Act, on which the indictment is founded, being in conflict with the 23rd section of the 10th Article of the constitution of this State. That section provides

'that the right of the citizens to bear arms in defense of themselves and the state shall not be questioned'....

That the provisions of the Act in question do not import an entire destruction of the right of the citizens to bear arms in defense of themselves and the State will not be controverted by the court; for though the citizens are forbid wearing weapons concealed in the manner described in the Act, they may nevertheless bear arms in any other admissable form. But to be in conflict with the constitution it is not essential that the act should contain a prohibition against bearing arms in every form...whatever constrains the full and complete exercise of that right, although not an entire destruction of it, is forbidden by the explicit language of the constitution.

(Bliss v. Commonwealth, 12 Ky. 90 (1822))

69. EXERCISE OF THE RIGHT AS SUBJECT TO REGULATION: LOUISIANA UPHOLDS A SIMILAR STATUTE

A ban on concealed weapons carrying fared better in the Louisiana Court of Appeals. The court did not doubt that the right to bear arms applied to individual citizens, but took the view that the statute did not infringe that right since it would still be possible to bear arms, so long as they were not concealed.

This law became absolutely necessary to counteract a vicious habit of society, growing out of the habit of carrying concealed weapons.... It interferes with no man's right to carry arms (to use its words) 'in full open view,' which places men upon an equality. This is a right guaranteed by the Constitution of the United States, and which is calculated to incite men to a manly and noble defense of themselves, if necessary, and of their country, without any tendency to secret advantages....

(State v. Chandler, 5 La. App. 489, 52 Am. Dec. 599 (1850))

70. REGULATION HAS LIMITS: ALABAMA UPHOLDS CONCEALED CARRY RESTRICTIONS, WITH A CAVEAT

When the Alabama Supreme Court upheld a concealed carrying ban in 1840 it added a warning that its decision should not be read to allow such regulation of arms bearing as would destroy the right to bear arms. Perhaps the court was mindful of a recently-enacted handgun prohibition in neighboring Georgia, discussed in the next section.

> The Constitution, in declaring that every citizen has the right to bear arms in defense of himself and the state, has neither expressly nor by implication denied to the legislature the right to enact laws in regard to the manner in which arms shall be borne.
>
> We do not desire to be understood as maintaining, that in regulating the manner of wearing arms, the legislature has no other limit than its own discretion. A statute which, under the pretence of regulating, amounts to a destruction of the right, or which requires arms to be so borne as to render them wholly useless for the purpose of defense, would be clearly unconstitutional.

(State v. Reid, 1 Ala. 612 (1840))

71. EXCEEDING THE LIMITS: GEORGIA VOIDS A HANDGUN BAN

Those who consider handgun bans a novel approach may be suprised to learn that on December 25, 1837, Georgia enacted a statute banning all private possession of certain weapons, including pistols. Georgia at the time had no right to bear arms guarantee in its constitution. Yet in Nunn v. State, its Supreme Court held the statute violative of the second amendment to the federal constitution. This is all the more extraordinary, since the United States Supreme Court had already ruled, in Barron v. Baltimore, that the federal bill of rights did not restrict state actions. Today, the court's result seems unusual to most legal minds. It may not have seemed so when it was genuinely believed that the concepts we call 'rights' were inherent in the individual—that a constitution might 'recognize' them, but did not 'create' them. After all, if the rights are 'unalienable'—the 18th century terms for 'non-transferable'—should it make a difference whether a state or a federal government is the one claiming to have been transferred the power over the right in question?

It is true, that these adjudications (in earlier concealed weapons cases) were all made upon clauses in the state constitutions; but these instruments confer no new rights on people which did not belong to them before. When, I would ask, did any legislative body in the Union have the right to deny to its citizens the privilege of keeping and bearing arms in defense of themselves and their country? If this right, 'inestimable to free men,' has been guaranteed to British subjects since the flight of the last of the Stuarts and the ascention of the Prince of Orange, did it not belong to our colonial ancestors in the western hemisphere?...(T)his is one of the fundamental principles upon which rests the great fabric of civil liberty....

I am inclined to the opinion that the article in question does extend to all judicial tribunals, whether constituted by the Congress of the United States or the states individually.... Does it follow that, because the people refused to delegate to the general government the power to take away from them their right to keep and bear arms, they designed to rest it in the state government? Is this a right reserved to the States or to themselves? Is it not an inalienable right, which lies at the bottom of every free government?...

The right of whole people, old and young, men, women and boys, and not militia only, to keep and bear arms of every description, and not such merely as are used by the militia, shall not be infringed...in the slightest degree; and all this for the important end to be attained, the rearing up and qualifying a well-regulated militia, so vitally necessary to a free state.

(Nunn v. State, 1 Ga. 243 (1846))

TO KEEP AND BEAR ARMS
IN THE SUPREME COURT

72. RIGHT OF CITIZENS TO "CARRY ARMS WHEREVER THEY WENT": DRED SCOTT v. SANFORD

Few decisions are as unusual as Dred Scott. The plaintiff's name was not really Dred Scott; he did not want to be freed (being elderly and ill, he would likely starve); his 'owner' wanted slavery abolished and brought this as a test case. Justice Taney's opinion meant to uphold slavery, but did much to ensure the election of Lincoln, the outbreak of the Civil War, and slavery's elimination. In one portion of the lengthy opinion, the Supreme Court argued that the states adopting the Constitution could not have meant to consider even free blacks as citizens, and outlined the rights which black Americans would have if given citizenship.

> More especially, it cannot be believed that the large slaveholding states regarded them as included in the word 'citizens' or would have consented to a constitution which might compel them to receive them in that character from another state. For if they were so received, and entitled to the privileges and immunities of citizens....(i)t would give to citizens of the negro race, who were recognized as citizens in any one state of the Union, the right to enter every other state wherever they pleased, singly or in companies, without pass or passport....and it would give to them the full liberty of speech in public and in private, upon all subjects upon which its own citizens might speak; to hold public meetings upon political affairs, and to keep and carry arms wherever they went.

(Dred Scott v. Sanford, 60 U.S. 393, 420 (1856))

73. RIGHTS TO ASSEMBLE, AND TO BEAR ARMS, NOT 'GRANTED' BY THE CONSTITUTION: U.S. v. CRUIKSHANK

Cruikshank is certainly one of the most often misconstrued decisions of the Supreme Court—probably because it involves some of the Court's most obscure reasoning. Before the Civil War, the U.S. Supreme Court had held the federal Bill of Rights to bind only the federal government, not the states. Following that war, the 14th Amendment was ratified, which provided in part that "no state shall make or enforce any law which shall abridge the privileges or immunities of citizens of the United States, nor shall any state deprive any person of life, liberty or property without due process of law." Congress enacted "Enforcement Acts," punishing conspiracies to abridge these privileges and immunities. The Supreme Court chose, however, to take a very narrow view of these enactments. It held that rights which persons had as natural rights, before the establishment of the United States, could not be "privileges...of citizens of the United States." Thus the most vital rights were read out of the Enforcement Acts. To the very extent that a right was found inherent to humanity—to the extent citizens could argue they had been "endowed by their Creator" with a given 'unalienable right'—Cruikshank held that right unprotected by the Enforcement Acts. In Cruikshank, state officials were prosecuted for conspiring to break up and disarm a meeting of black citizens—and the Court held their action legal!

> This case...presents for our consideration an indictment...based upon section six of the Enforcement Act (which) is as follows: 'That if two or more persons should band or conspire together...to injure, oppress, threaten or intimidate any citizen, with intent to prevent or hinder his free exercise and enjoyment of any right or privilege granted or secured to him by the constitution or laws of the United States...such persons shall be held guilty of felony....'
>
> To bring this case under the operation of the statute, therefore, it must appear that the right, the enjoyment of which the conspirators intended to hinder or prevent, was one granted or secured by the constitution or laws of the United States.... We have in our political system a government of the United States and a government of each of the several states....
>
> The first and ninth counts state the intent of the defendants to have been to hinder and prevent the citizens named in the free exercise and enjoyment of their 'lawful and privilege to peaceably assemble together...for a lawful purpose.' The right of the people peaceably to assemble for lawful purposes existed long before the adoption of the Constitution of the United States. In fact, it is and has always been one of the attributes of citizenship under a free government.... It was not, therefore, a right granted to the people by the Constitution. The government of the United States when established found it in existence....

The second and tenth counts are equally defective. The right there specified is that of 'bearing arms for a lawful purpose.' This is not a right granted by the Constitution. Neither is it in any manner dependent upon that instrument for its existence....

The third and eleventh counts are even more objectionable. They charge the intent to have been to deprive the citizens named, they being in Louisiana, 'of their respective several lives and liberty of person without due process of law.' This is nothing more than alleging a conspiracy to falsely imprison or murder citizens of the United States.... the rights of life and personal liberty are the natural rights of man....

The order of the Circuit Court arresting the judgement upon the verdict is, therefore, affirmed: and the cause remanded, with instructions to discharge the defendants.

(United States v. Cruikshank, 92 U.S. 542 (1876))

74. STATE LAW AND THE FEDERAL MILITIA: PRESSER v. ILLINOIS

Today, few persons would care to accept Cruikshank's position that a conspiracy of state officials aimed at restricting freedom of speech and assembly and murdering minorities does not violate the 14th amendment or federal civil rights statutes. Presser v. Illinois involved a more unusual prosecution. Herman Presser was leader of a German-American group known as the Lehr und Wehr Verein, which appears to have been a pro-labor group organized in response to violent strikebreaking tactics. In 1879, while carrying an officer's sword, he led the group on parade through Chicago. He was prosecuted under a state law which, while not limiting arms ownership, barred unlicensed military drilling while armed. After paying a $10 fine, he appealed, arguing that the statute violated the Second Amendment and also the 1792 Militia Act, which required most male citizens to own a firearm.

We think it clear that the sections under consideration, which only forbid bodies of men to associate together as military organizations, or to drill or parade with arms in cities and towns unless authorized by law, do not infringe the right of the people to keep and bear arms. But a conclusive answer to the contention that this Amendment prohibits the legislation in question lies in the fact that the amendment is a limitation only upon the powers of Congress and the National Government, and not upon that of the States. It was so held by this Court in the case of United States v. Cruikshank (quoting from the opinion).

It is undoubtedly true that all citizens capable of bearing arms constitute the reserved military force or reserved militia of the United States as well as of the States, and in view of this prerogative of the general government, as well as of its general powers, the states cannot, even laying the constitutional provision in question out of view, prohibit the people from keeping and bearing arms, so as to deprive the United States of their rightful resource for maintaining the public security, and disable the people from performing their duty to the general government. But, as already stated, we think it clear that the sections under consideration do not have this effect.

(Presser v. Illinois, 116 U.S. 252 (1886))

75. EXPLANATION WITHOUT CLARIFICATION: U.S. v. MILLER

During the first century and a half of the Bill of Rights, the Supreme Court thus did little but debate where the second amendment was applicable. Except for the brief comment in Dred Scott, no clarification was given as to what the second amendment did forbid where it applied. In 1939, the Court issued its one and only decision in the latter area and, unfortunately, the ambiguous ruling promptly joined Cruikshank on the list of understandably misconstrued rulings. Congress had in 1934 enacted the National Firearms Act, which required payment of a $200 tax (and consequent registration) before transfer of a machinegun or sawed-off rifle or shotgun. When one Jack Miller was arrested and charged with acquiring a sawed-off shotgun without such payment, the trial court dismissed the charge. That court took no evidence and simply held that the National Firearms Act violated the second amendment as a matter of law. The United States appealed. Miller was apparently too poor to retain an attorney for the appeal, so the appeal was presented on the government's brief alone. The Supreme Court simply held that the trial court erred in not taking evidence as to the nature of the weapon. While a court might take 'judicial notice' of indisputable facts—such as whether a given date fell on a Monday, or the location of a state capital—it could not take notice of so general a question as whether a sawed-off shotgun was appropriate to militia-related skills. The Court did not hold that Miller had no second amendment argument—it merely remanded for further consideration. Unfortunately for legal historians, Miller vanished while the case was on appeal. One thing which can be said of the case is this: the Miller decision emphatically did not hold that the second amendment only protects National Guard units. If that were so, there was no need for the decision or the remand; no one ever claimed Jack Miller was a member of a reserve unit. 'National Guard' is not even mentioned in the opinion. The test seems instead to focus upon the arm involved—and only to require a showing of 'some reasonable relationship' to the efficiency of a militia, which consists of all citizens capable of bearing arms. The opinion further implies that the test may be whether the weapon in question is one 'in common use' among citizens; if this is so, the remand for additional evidence is understandable, as is the Court's emphasis upon Miller's being charged with possessing a sawed-off shotgun as opposed to a more ordinary firearm.

In the absence of any evidence tending to show that the possession or use of a 'shotgun having a barrel of less than eighteen inches in length' at this time has some reasonable relationship to the preservation or efficiency of a well regulated militia, we cannot say that the second amendment guarantees the right to keep and bear such an instrument. Certainly it is not within judicial notice that this weapon is any part of the ordinary military equipment or that its use could contribute to the common defense.(citation).

The Constitution as originally adopted granted to the Congress power to 'provide for calling forth the Militia....' With obvious purpose to assure the continuation and render possible the effectiveness of such forces the declaration and guarantee of the second amendment were made. It must be interpreted and applied with that end in view.

The militia which the States were expected to maintain and train is set in contrast with the troops which they were forbidden to keep without consent of Congress. The sentiment of the time strongly disfavored standing armies; the common view was that adequate defense of country and laws could be secured through the militia—civilians primarily, soldiers on occasion.

The signification attached to the term militia appears from the debates in the Convention, the history and legislation of the colonies and states, and the writings of approved commentators. These show plainly enough that the militia comprised all males physically capable of acting in concert for the common defense. 'A body of citizens enrolled for military discipline' (citations). And, further, that ordinarily when called for service, these men were expected to appear bearing arms supplied by themselves and of the kind in common use at the time.... This implied the general obligation of all adult male inhabitants to possess arms, and, with certain exceptions, to cooperate in the work of defense. The possession of arms also implied the possession of ammunition, and authorities paid quite as much attention to the latter as to the former.

(United States v. Miller, 307 U.S. 174 (1939))